I0637302

Faces of Stones River

Daniel A. Masters

Columbian Arsenal Press
Perrysburg, Ohio

First Printing: 2025

ISBN: 978-1-300-55795-1

Columbian Arsenal Press
Perrysburg, Ohio 43551
https://columbianarsenal.com/
Email: Columbianarsenal@gmail.com

Table of Accounts and Images

Major William F. Douglass, 6th/7th Arkansas Consolidated Infantry

Private William F. Shores, Co. H, 6th/7th Arkansas Infantry

Second Lieutenant John L. Mitchell, aide-de-camp to General Sill

Brigadier General Joshua W. Sill, commanding 1st Brigade, 3rd Division, McCook's Wing

Private Samuel Seay, Co. C, 1st Tennessee Infantry

Private Sam Watkins, Co. H, 1st Tennessee Infantry

Private Thomas J. Maxwell, Co. C, 42nd Illinois Infantry

Captain Wesley P. Andrus, Co. H, 42nd Illinois Infantry

Lieutenant C. Irvine Walker, assistant adjutant general to Colonel Manigault

First Lieutenant John R. Ellis, Co. I, 19th South Carolina Infantry

Captain Charles Houghtaling, Battery C, 1st Illinois Light Artillery

Captain Charles Houghtaling, Battery C, 1st Illinois Light Artillery

Major General Benjamin F. Cheatham, Cheatham's Div., Polk's Corps

Major General Benjamin F. Cheatham, Cheatham's Div., Polk's Corps

Sergeant Launcelot Scott, Co. G, 18th Ohio Infantry

Sergeant Launcelot Scott, Co. G, 18th Ohio Infantry

Captain Andrew J. Jones, Co. C, 27th Mississippi Infantry

Private James M. Fear, Co. K, 27th Mississippi Infantry

Ordnance Sergeant Adoniram J. Hastings, 78th Pennsylvania Infantry

78th Pennsylvania soldiers stop Lookout Mountain

Brigadier General Alexander P. Stewart

Private L.A. Morphis, Co. F, 5th Tennessee Infantry

Colonel Thomas D. Sedgewick, 2nd Kentucky Infantry (U.S.)

Private Amos Hussey, Co. F, 2nd Kentucky Infantry (U.S.)

Captain Simon Mayer, volunteer aide to General James R. Chalmers

Members of Co. B, 9th Mississippi Infantry

Private Thomas B. Beall, Co. I, 10th Mississippi Infantry

Private Almon Stuart, Co. I, 9th Indiana Infantry

Sergeant Horace Marble, Co. E, 9th Indiana Infantry

Lieutenant Colonel John H. Anderson, 8th Tennessee Infantry

Colonel William L. Moore, 8th Tennessee Infantry

Sergeant Henry Breidenthal, Co. A, 3rd Ohio Infantry

Private Owen E. Moore, Co. B, 3rd Ohio Infantry

Private Lycurgus A. Sallee, Co. C, 1st Arkansas Infantry

Brigadier General Lucius E. Polk, commanding Polk's Brigade, Cleburne's Div.

Sergeant Frank Reed, Co. H, 1st Battalion, 15th U.S. Infantry
Captain J. Bowman Bell, Co. D, 1st Battalion, 15th U.S. Infantry
Brigadier General John A. Wharton
Private Ed Landvoigt, Co. I, 1st Confederate Cavalry
Captain Martin Buck, Co. H, 1st Ohio Cavalry
Colonel John Minor Millikin, 1st Ohio Cavalry
Brigadier General Sterling A.M. Wood
First Lieutenant Isaac C. Madding, Co. B, 16th Alabama Infantry
Major Charles Manderson, 19th Ohio Infantry
Major Charles Manderson, 19th Ohio Infantry
Colonel Alfred J. Vaughan
Colonel Alfred J. Vaughan, commanding Vaughan's Brigade, Cheatham's Div.
First Lieutenant Marvin B. Butler, Co. A, 44th Indiana Infantry
Companies G and H, 44th Indiana Infantry in May 1864
Captain William H. Harder, Co. D, 23rd Tennessee Infantry
Private Allen B. Pollock, Co. B, 23rd Tennessee Infantry
Second Lieutenant Wilbur F. Hinman, Co. E, 65th Ohio Infantry
Second Lieutenant Wilbur F. Hinman, Co. E, 65th Ohio Infantry
Brigadier General St. John R. Liddell
Brigadier General St. John R. Liddell, commanding Liddell's Brigade, Cleburne's Div.
Captain Frederick Garternicht, Co. G, 84th Illinois Infantry
Captain Frederick Garternicht, Co. G, 84th Illinois Infantry
Lieutenant General William J. Hardee, Hardee's Corps
Lieutenant General William J. Hardee, commanding Hardee's Corps
Captain Henry Haymond, Co. E, 3rd Battalion, 18th U.S. Infantry
Captain Henry Haymond, Co. E, 3rd Battalion, 18th U.S. Infantry
Captain William A. Cotter, Co. H, 30th Arkansas Infantry
Captured colors of 30th Arkansas Infantry
Sergeant Tobias Ross, Co. B, 2nd Ohio Infantry
Private Alexander G. Walker, Co. I, 2nd Ohio Infantry
Colonel Julius A. Andrews, 15th Texas Cavalry (Dismounted)
Colonel Julius A. Andrews, 15th Texas Cavalry (Dismounted)
Private Charles H. Maple, Chicago Board of Trade Battery
Federal gunners loading a cannon

Captain Ezekiel John Ellis, Co. E, 16th Louisiana Infantry
Private James N. Murphy, Co. E, 16th Louisiana Infantry
George H. Woodruff, regimental historian, 100th Illinois Infantry
Colonel Frederick A. Bartleson, 100th Illinois Infantry
Colonel Randall L. Gibson, 13th/20th Louisiana Infantry
Colonel Randall L. Gibson, 13th/20th Louisiana Infantry
Adjutant Edwin Nicar, 15th Indiana Infantry
Captain Joel W. Foster, Co. G, 15th Indiana Infantry
Major General Patrick R. Cleburne
Major General Patrick R. Cleburne, commanding Cleburne's Div., Hardee's Corps
Colonel Michael Shoemaker, 13th Michigan Infantry
Colonel Michael Shoemaker, 13th Michigan Infantry
Sergeant William D. Rodgers, Co. K, 1st Florida Infantry
Colonel William Miller, 1st/3rd Consolidated Florida Infantry
Second Lieutenant Augustus O. McDonnell, Co. K, 1st/3rd Florida Infantry
Colonel William Grose, Third Brigade, First Division, Left Wing
Colonel William Grose, Third Brigade, First Division, Left Wing
Colonel Joseph B. Palmer, Palmer's Brigade, Breckinridge's Div.
Colonel Joseph B. Palmer, Palmer's Brigade, Breckinridge's Div.
Captain James B. Stinchcomb, Co. B, 17th Ohio Infantry
Captain Ezra Ricketts, Co. F, 17th Ohio Infantry
Major William D. Pickett, Assistant Inspector General, Hardee's Corps
Major General John C. Breckinridge, commanding Breckinridge's Division, Hardee's Corps
Sergeant John H. Purvis, Co. B, 51st Ohio Infantry
Sergeant John H. Purvis, Co. B, 51st Ohio Infantry
Sergeant Dan Turney, Co. G, 2nd Kentucky Infantry (C.S.A.)
Brigadier General Robert W. Hanson, commanding Hanson's Brigade, Breckinridge's Div.
Adjutant Erasmus D. Thomas, 86th Indiana Infantry
Private George E. Armer, Co. B, 86th Indiana Infantry
Captain Theodorick "Tod" Carter, Co. H, 20th Tennessee Infantry
Private Francis M. Battle, Co. B, 20th Tennessee Infantry
First Lieutenant Robert S. Dilworth, Co. I, 21st Ohio Infantry
First Lieutenant Robert S. Dilworth, Co. I, 21st Ohio Infantry
Brigadier General Gideon J. Pillow, Palmer's Brigade, Breckinridge's Division
Brigadier General Gideon J. Pillow, Palmer's Brigade, Breckinridge's Division

Captain John Mendenhall, chief of artillery, Left Wing
Major General Thomas L. Crittenden, commanding Left Wing
Colonel John G. Coltart, 26th Alabama Infantry
Colonel John G. Coltart, 26th Alabama Infantry
Lieutenant Colonel James M. Shanklin, 42nd Indiana Infantry
Lieutenant Colonel James M. Shanklin, 42nd Indiana Infantry
Sergeant Isaac Wark, Co. E, 1st Louisiana Regular Infantry
Major General Jones M. Withers, Wither's Div., Polk's Corps
Colonel John Beatty, Second Brigade, First Division, Center Corps
Colonel John Beatty, Second Brigade, First Division, Center Corps

It was the hard task of the loved ones left behind North and South to carry on with the rigors of daily life despite the extended absences of their soldier boys in blue and gray. Above, an unidentified Confederate had his "likeness" taken at Corinth, Mississippi early in the war and paired with the woman at left, probably a sister. Colonel George P. Buell of the 58th Indiana, a first cousin of General Don Carlos Buell, is shown below with his sister Alma Buell, both residents of Dearborn County, Indiana.

Introduction

The Battle of Stones River, Tennessee ranks as one of the hardest fought and bloodiest engagements of the Civil War. Between December 30, 1862, and January 3, 1863, the 37,000 men of the Army of Tennessee led by General Braxton Bragg and 44,000 men of the Army of the Cumberland under General William S. Rosecrans struggled for control of middle Tennessee in a see-saw fight that eventually resulted in both a narrow Union victory and more than 25,000 casualties. Stones River proved a crucial and timely Union victory in the midst of significant military setbacks during what could be considered the North's lowest point of the war.

Both armies recuperated for months following the battle which gave the participants ample time to record their impressions of this sanguinary conflict. What follows in this volume are accounts from 72 soldiers, about equally split between Federal and Confederate perspectives, that focus on the primary actions fought at Stones River on December 31, 1862, and January 2, 1863. The accounts are arranged in chronological order and follow the general progression of the battle as it developed. The perspectives are diverse, ranging from the highest-ranking generals to regimental commanders, down to line officers and enlisted men in the ranks.

To enhance these accounts, I have assembled photographs to accompany each account, depicting either the soldier himself, someone in his unit, or in his chain of command. The hope is that by combining these images and words, the reader will come away with a deeper appreciation of the human and visual experiences of the battle and spark further interest in studying this important campaign.

Over 81,000 men participated in the Battle of Stones River and every one of them had a story to tell. Here are a few of them…

Daniel A. Masters
February 20, 2025

Lieutenant General Braxton Bragg, commanding the Army of Tennessee

Major General William Starke Rosecrans, commanding the Army of the Cumberland

"It would have been impossible for me to save my battery"

Captain Warren P. Edgarton, Battery E, 1st Ohio Light Artillery

At daylight a small stream was discovered about 100 rods in our rear. It was quiet all along our lines. I could not hear a picket shot, nor any indication that the enemy was in our vicinity. I had no orders to take position. My horses were already harnessed, to hitch on at a moment's warning. I was completely surrounded by veteran troops. I had a right to suppose that our front and flank were so picketed that I should have notice of the approach of the enemy.

I ordered a half battery of my horses to go to water on a sharp trot and return at the slightest indication of danger. The horses had barely reached the water when a fierce shout was heard at the front, and a terrible volley of musketry was poured in upon us. I called the cannoneers to their posts, had a half battery hitched in, put my guns in battery where they were, and a moment was prepared, as best I could, to fight in that position. The infantry, our support, gave way on the front and flank in disorder, almost with the first volley. I then opened on the enemy with canister, firing from 16 to 20 rounds, with good effect, as I have cause to know, for I passed over the ground in our front a few moments afterward a prisoner.

The assault of the enemy was fierce and overwhelming. After the first fire, in which I had one man killed, a number wounded, and twelve horses killed, the enemy charged with an impetuosity which carried everything before him. The battery was taken. It would have been impossible for me to have saved my battery, even if I had commenced a retreat on the first alarm. The enemy was very near us before discovered, and the fight commenced without any of the preliminary skirmishing before a general engagement. To the best of my judgment, it was not more than five minutes from the firing of the first shot to the catastrophe when my battery was taken and myself a prisoner.

Captain Warren Parker Edgarton commanded Battery E, 1ˢᵗ Ohio Light Artillery and was wounded twice then captured among his guns at dawn on December 31, 1862. He spent the next five months in captivity.
(Author's Collection)

"Many a pot of Rio coffee was run over or left to boil out."

Lt. Col. Joseph Murray Bounds, 11th Texas Cavalry (Dismounted)

At light the left wing of our army, consisting of the Texas Brigade commanded by General Matthew D. Ector and the Arkansas brigade commanded by General Evander McNair, charged the enemy's stronghold, routed, and chased them about three miles leaving the ground over which we passed strewed with dead and wounded Yankees from the grade of brigadier general down to a private.

When the charge was called off there was not a Fed to be seen except some cavalry that were making their way to a cedar brake on a double quick and the infantry that had not fell or been captured and thrown off their knapsacks, and all the baggage and dispersed in the hills and thick woods. When we made the charge, we took them by surprise and made them leave their breakfast on the fires and many a hundred pot of Rio coffee was run over or left to boil out.

First Lt. Josiah Taylor Tunnell, Co. B, 14th Texas Cavalry (Dismounted)

When we struck their skirmish line in the open field, we drove them back on their main line so rapidly that we got to within easy gunshot of their main line before they knew it. My regiment confronted a battery of six guns…but they fired only two or three shots until we were among them.

Many of the Yanks were either killed or retreated in their nightclothes. We found a caisson with the horses attached lodged against a tree and other evidence of their confusion. The Yanks tried to make a stand whenever they could find shelter of any kind. All along our route we captured prisoners, who would take refuge behind houses, fences, logs, cedar bushed and in ravines. We drove them helter-skelter about three miles when we halted to reform at the south side of a small open field, beyond which was a heavy grove of timber, mostly red cedar, into which the enemy had retreated.

Third Lieutenant John Alonzo Beall of Co. D of the 14th Texas Cavalry (Dismounted)
poses while holding a Sharps rifle in August 1861. At Stones River, the 14th Texas, part of
General Mathew D. Ector's all Texas brigade, launched the initial assault on the Federal
right and suffered the loss of 74 casualties.
(Liljenquist Collection)

"The enemy charged in five lines yelling like Indians"
Private Noah Webster Downs, Co. D, 39th Indiana Infantry

On the night of the 30th of December, Co. D with other companies of the

39th were on picket. Our company joined the pickets of Kirk's brigade at right angles, their pickets fronting to our left. Early the following morning, firing commenced in front of Kirk's pickets. They gradually gave way, leaving our left entirely exposed. Colonel Fielder Jones, as soon as he was apprised of this fact, ordered Co. D to fall back and join the brigade again. But no sooner done than the Rebels came over a hill charging bayonets and yelling like Indians. Their line was five columns deep. Now what was to be done?

The evening before, Colonel Jones had ordered us to hold that line at all hazards. The balls were flying thick and fast; our support on the left had retreated and we were left all alone. Colonel Jones rode between us and the Rebs and ordered us to retreat. This was done in good order as long as there was any chance, but the Rebs pressed too close to be comfortable and we had to execute a military movement which is very disagreeable in our drill but became very necessary on that day. Colonel Jones was at all times where the balls flew thickest- his voice could be heard above the din of battle trying to rally his men. The next morning, he collected all he could of the once proud 39th Indiana which was just 120 men!

In the retreat on Wednesday, Captain Herring with several of his men was captured. The guard having charge of them ordered him to double quick but Herring told him, in his peculiar way, that he had "quit doing that." The guard, much enraged, drew a revolver and swore he would shoot him. "Shoot and be damned," said Herring. "I'm tired." About this time, our cavalry made a dash on the Rebs which allowed Herring to turn to his guard and say "Sir, this changes the program. You dismount and take off that saber!" The fellow wilted, got off, and held the horse while the captain mounted. What a change!

*Corporal William Stanley of Co. D, 39th Indiana Infantry, posing here with a non-
commissioned officer's sword in a postwar cabinet card which utilized a wartime image,
suffered a severe wound in his left leg near the knee and died of that wound January 9, 1863,
in Murfreesboro. His cousin Lieutenant Josiah Stanley commanded Co. D at Stones River
and was slightly wounded in the neck.
(Find-A-Grave)*

"Doing a thriving six-shooter business"

First Lt. Benjamin Franklin Batchelor, Co. C, 8th Texas Cavalry

Daylight had hardly broke on the memorable 31st when Ector's Texas brigade and Wharton's cavalry were in rapid motion towards the enemy. Soon the charge was ordered and it would have made a heart of stone leap with enthusiasm to see the gallant boys double quacking with shining bayonets while the Bonnie Blue flag proudly fluttered in the breeze and a long simultaneous yell reverberated along the lines. As the ripened grain bends before the driving blast of the mower's sickle, so the Abolition hordes fell before the charge. In 20 minutes, we had captured several fine batteries and had the enemy's right wing turned and in full flight.

Their cavalry showed us their backs and we were running after them with the speed of a steeple chase. By dint of great exertion, their cavalry rallied to support a battery planted to protect their train of wagons then retiring towards Nashville. Captain Samuel P. Christian with four companies (including Co. C) charged the battery and took one rifled Parrott gun. In this affair, it affords me pleasure to say that George fought by the captain's side and received his warm commendation before the command in these words: "George, by God, you're a trump! You'll do to tie to, old fellow!"

When near the enemy's wagons, the cavalry made another stand and the Georgia regiment was ordered to charge them, which they did in good style but the Yankees outnumbered them and drove them back. An exciting scene presented itself: the poor Georgians who were mostly armed with long Enfield rifles and nothing else had fired and being unable to load in the face of an advancing fore had turned and with heads stretching forward like turkeys in a drive were kicking their horses for dear life while Mr. Yankee had drawn his shining swords and was bending forward in hot pursuit making the air whiz with saber cuts close upon the Georgians.

It needed no word to charge. The boys went in pell-mell and were soon thinning the enemy's lines and doing a thriving six-shooter business when Mr. Yankee turned and fled in utter confusion. We drove them through their train and a mile beyond it and captured about 400 wagons and 800 prisoners, but unfortunately, we carried the pursuit too far.

Adjutant James T. Walker of the 8th Texas Cavalry, also known as Terry's Texas Rangers. The regiment, on outpost duty near Nolensville protecting the left of the Army of Tennessee at the beginning of the campaign, saw action repeatedly in the days leading up the main fighting on December 31, 1862, then played a crucial role during the Confederate assaults on the Union right.

"The temptation to throw away my gun was great"

Sergeant George R. Bradshaw, Co. F, 74th Illinois Infantry

This was the first time the regiment had been under fire and they felt very

uneasy as the shells came hissing along several came pretty close to me nearer than I liked. I could see them coming through the air as plainly as one can see a ball thrown from the hand. One passed over my head knocking off the top of a fence stake and striking the ground twenty feet behind me bounded again and burst in the woods behind. No one was hurt and in 20 minutes our guns had driven off the Secesh battery.

Our regiment made several stands. As the Secesh came up, we dealt death to them but they were three to our one and we had to give way. It really seems a miracle how anyone can come out alive from such a storm of bullets and grape shot as we were in the 74th lost many men. Three men from Co. F were wounded, several more we suppose killed but we can hear nothing of them as the Rebs had the field and the dead in their possession.

The retreat all this day reminded me of what Bull Run must have been. Ambulances and wagons rushed through the forest and fields pell-mell the men lashing their horses to the top of their speed. Many of the soldiers threw away their guns, blankets, coats, and everything and ran with speed towards Nashville many did not stop until they were safe inside the entrenchments 30 miles from the field of battle.

Johnson's entire division was in wild flight and much of Davis's in which is the 74th Illinois. As for my part, I hung on my gun and all I had. The temptation to throw away my gun and run was great but I thought that a little too cowardly even for me so I kept near the front and did the Rebs all the damage I could.

*Sergeant Franklin W. Fuller, Co. I, 74th Illinois Infantry
(Austin Sundstrom Collection)*

"The regiment moved up in fine style under a galling fire"

Lt. Col. Watt W. Floyd, 17th Tennessee Infantry

The regiment was led into action by the gallant Colonel Albert Smith Marks.

When the brigade was in position to move against the enemy's lines, the 17th Tennessee occupied a position in a bottom, where a battery had been captured a few minutes before by General McCown's command. Upon being ordered forward, the regiment advanced up a gentle slope to a fence on the crest of the hill. Here our skirmishers were first fired upon, and we discovered a heavy force supporting a battery in a cornfield immediately in front of our lines.

The regiment moved up in fine style to within 150 yards of the battery, under a galling fire from the artillery and infantry. We halted and engaged them for some length of time to great effect. Colonel Marks was wounded here at the first fire, and the command then devolved upon me. The enemy's line finally gave way, and the order was given to charge. Never did soldiers obey an order with more alacrity. We captured the battery and drove the enemy back to the edge of a thick woodland. After passing the battery, we halted and engaged the enemy a second time, soon starting him back again. I ordered a second charge, which was well executed under a heavy fire. On gaining the fence from which we had just driven the enemy, I reformed the regiment. Here the enemy made a very stubborn stand, taking shelter behind the trees and logs; here my left suffered severely from an enfilading fire.

The enemy's line had not given way on my left. He occupied the opposite side of the fence from me, not exceeding 60 yards from me. Colonel Richard H. Keeble, with his noble little band (23rd Tennessee Infantry), came soon to our relief, with General St. John Liddell on his left. I discovered that the right wing of the brigade was still held in check some distance in our rear by the enemy, strongly posted in a wood in front of it; but my men were so anxious to go forward that I ordered them to clear the wood in front. So soon as I saw the enemy's line break to my left, we kept up a running and a very destructive fire through the wood, which was, perhaps, some 300 yards.

Private Charles Wesley Sadler, Co. K, 17ᵗʰ Tennessee Infantry was among the men of General Bushrod Johnson's brigade who battled with Colonel P. Sidney Post's men along Gresham Lane. Slightly wounded in the leg during the battle, he poses here holding a Model 1841 Mississippi rifle with a Starr revolver tucked into his belt.
(Tennessee Confederate Images)

"I think my first shot went nearly straight into the air"
Private Charles Barney Dennis, Co. B, 101st Ohio Infantry

Our position went against us immediately after the battle opened up the next day or early morning. We had had such breakfast as we could get at 5 o'clock and then lay there watching the heavy lines of infantry that the Rebels were pushing around to our extreme right. We could see the battle flags plainly but were not allowed to fire at them. About half past five a line of skirmishers was pushed forward by the Rebels and it promptly commenced picking on us. It was followed, as we found just a little later, by two heavy lines of battle, just twice our strength.

When these rebel skirmishers began shooting, we were ordered into line, standing like a wall of human beings for them to pick off. Still the order to came to us, 'hold your fire, men! Give way to the right, give way to the left, steady, steady.' All this time we heard the thud of bullets as they found their way into some poor fellow's flesh and the falling men all along the line were easily seen as they pitched forward on their faces, many of them never to rise again. Finally, their skirmishers came out of the bushes a little, keeping up a steady fusillade but it was then that we could see what was behind that skirmish line. Soon after we received the order to fire. At first, we were ordered to deliver volley firing, then came the order 'fire at will and fire low, aim at their knees!' We could see their knees as they came on and we did aim at them, although I think the first shot I fired went very nearly straight up in the air, and if my recollection serves me, it must have taken a sort of curve up and over the Rebel line and fallen on the other side. I hope to this day that it had some effect on some Johnny.

Owing to the fact that the Rebels outnumbered us nearly two to one, at least on the right wing of our army, we were compelled to fall back slowly, changing our front slightly and facing more to the east as we were now in the crook of the elbow so to speak of the Rebel force. They were attempting an enveloping movement which, if successful, would put our whole army in a very dangerous position. But by the prompt action of some of the division commanders, especially General Sheridan and Davis, they were prevented, although they continued to drive our force back.

First Lieutenant Daniel Hillyer commanding Co. F of the 101st Ohio Volunteer Infantry was killed in action as his brigade fought against General S.A.M. Wood's Confederates amongst the trees and rock outcroppings east of Gresham Lane.
(Find-A-Grave)

"We charged with a yell, firing as we ran"

Private William E. Matthews Preston, Co. B, 33rd Alabama Infantry

We were laying in line of battle in a field the morning of December 31st,

ordered to load arms, then noiselessly advanced through the haze, as I remember, without skirmishers in front, could scarcely see a man 50 feet away. Soon found their line in a cedar thicket and charged with a yell, firing as we ran, breaking their line, and leaving their belongings such as breakfast on the fire, especially coffee, knapsacks, blankets, where they had been sleeping, shelter tents, guns and accoutrements and ambulances without the mules hooked u. We kept them going through the thickets on comparative level ground where they would at times make short stands behind trees, and rocks, then again in line, but would soon break, and flee, maybe across a clearing and form a line again, then break and fallback, leaving their wounded and dead with some cannon and many prisoners who were not wounded who greeted us as Buckner, not knowing Cleburne then had command, saying they knew us by our blue and white flags.

Colonel William Basil Wood, 16th Alabama Infantry

We continued to push on for more than half a mile, when we came upon

another line of the enemy. Again, a fierce and stubborn resistance was made. Again, the general ordered a charge, which was made with like results, the enemy being driven for more than half a mile until they fell behind a battery planted near a large frame house used as a hospital. Our line was reformed, and, with General Polk's brigade, moved up to charge the battery. As we approached, a few rounds were fired, and the battery was drawn off. We pursued as rapidly as possible, driving the enemy through the woods, across a cornfield, and beyond the Nolensville pike. As we approached the field another battery to our right opened upon us. We charged across this open field more than a quarter of a mile to capture the battery.

Private William Edward Davis of Co. C, 16th Alabama Infantry was severely wounded in the shoulder and captured a few days later when the Confederate army left Murfreesboro. (Find-A-Grave)

"A sheet of smoke and flame on our right"

Sergeant James K. Weir, Co. B, 25th Illinois Infantry

Early on Wednesday morning, the Rebels attacked the lines in great force and almost destroyed Johnson's division. Johnson was surprised and gave way, then came our turn. We stood it awhile then gave back. Here came the Rebels yelling like Indians, but we rallied and drove them back and retook our ground three times. The night prior, we had brought our knapsacks and laid them by a fence where we laid on our arms and there was a cornfield between us and the Rebels that they had to run across before they could reach us. They crossed over our knapsacks three times and had not disturbed them. By this time, there was a great many killed and wounded lying in the woods. Our colonel was killed also Daniel Dale; our captain John Burley was shot in the arm and we had several wounded the last time we ran them off.

I did not think they would bother us again but we saw the brigade on the right [Carlin's] falling back and the firing came nearer and directly it was one sheet of flame and smoke on our right. We had to run to save ourselves from being cut off. I did not know what the trouble was until we came into the cotton field; I gave out running and got behind the regiment and saw the whole line of battle running for life. I thought everything was lost, that it was a stampede and a Manassas affair. The Rebels followed closely, throwing shot and shell at us until we reached the timber where we formed lines again. They drove our lines so as to take possession of the road and captured a host of prisoners and wagons.

Private James G. Watson of Co. I, 25th Illinois Infantry in an image taken on December 10, 1862, at a studio in Nashville, Tennessee, just three weeks before Stones River. (Find-A-Grave)

"It looked for a time that all was lost"

Captain William P. Howell, Co. I, 25th Alabama Infantry

The enemy were posted in line of battle on the opposite side of a plantation from us some 800 yards and we advanced on them through the open field under heavy artillery fire as well as musketry and our loss was very heavy in going through the field. Four men, Sid Phillips, Gus Pool, Charly Roper and Jack Ezzell of Co. I were killed outright. Lieutenant Archibald Patterson of Co. H was also killed and every company of the regiment met a similar fate, in killed and wounded. Our line, in the face of their concentrated fire, got within 50 yards of their battery when our line gave way and stampeded back through the field and we suffered worse than while advancing.

Among the killed in that unfortunate stampede was Major Costello who had just been promoted from the Captaincy of Co. K. It looked for a time that all was lost and we had some difficulty in rallying the men and reforming the line of another attack. Lt. Scofield of Co. C from Columbiana was among the killed. I remember during the fight coming across his body just after he had fallen, he was shot dead. I stopped long enough to take a plain gold ring from his finger and his pocketknife and pocketbook and preserved them till after the battle and sent them home to his family.

I remember just at this critical moment General Frank Cheatham, Major General of Tennessee troops, came rushing to our aid. He made such a stirring appeal to the men, that our line was soon formed and in the face of another galling fire we charged on them again and so determined were the men that we rushed upon them and captured their battery and drove back the whole line, but they soon reformed their lines and for the live long day we fought over an area of two or three miles and at night fall we had driven them off the field.

At night fall, when the firing ceased, Lieutenant George D. Johnston was the only field officer with the regiment. I think I went in that morning with about 40 guns in Co. I and when the battle closed that night there was only one man, Pvt. Bob Clark and myself with the regiment. Most of the others had been either killed, wounded or captured.

Private Parris P. Casey, Co. I, 19th Alabama Infantry was with his fellow Alabamians of Colonel John Q. Loomis's brigade as they charged against Colonel William Woodruff's and General Joshua Sill's brigades east of Gresham Lane on the morning of December 31, 1862, at Stones River.
(Liljenquist Collection)

"The enemy fled in great confusion across the cotton field"

Captain Porter C. Olson, Co. F, 36th Illinois Infantry

On the morning of December 31, soon after daylight, the enemy advanced in strong force from the timber from beyond the cotton field opposite our right. They came diagonally across the field. Upon reaching the foot of the hill, they made a left half-wheel and came up directly in front of us. When the enemy had advanced up the hill sufficiently to be in sight, Colonel Nicholas Greusel ordered the regiment to fire, which was promptly obeyed. We engaged the enemy at short range, the lines being not over 10 rods apart. After a few rounds, the regiment supporting us on our right gave way. In this manner we fought for nearly half an hour, when Colonel Greusel ordered the regiment to charge. The enemy fled in great confusion across the cotton field into the woods opposite our left, leaving many of their dead and wounded upon the field. We poured a destructive fire upon them as they retreated until they were beyond range.

The 36th again took position upon the hill, and the support of our right came forward. At this time General Sill was killed, and Colonel Greusel took command of the brigade. A fresh brigade of the enemy advanced from the direction that the first had come, and in splendid order. We opened fire on them with terrific effect. Again, the regiment on our right gave way, and we were again left without support. In this condition we fought until our ammunition was exhausted, and until the enemy had entirely flanked us on our right. At this juncture Major Silas Miller ordered the regiment to fall back. While retreating, Major Miller was wounded, and the command devolved upon me. We moved back of the cornfield to the edge of the timber, a hundred rods to the right of the Wilkinson pike and two miles from Murfreesboro, at 8 a.m. Here I met General Sheridan and reported to him that the regiment was out of ammunition, and that I would be ready for action as soon as I could obtain it. We had suffered severely in resisting the attack of superior numbers. I had now only 140 men. The regiment fought with great obstinacy, and much is due to Colonel Nicholas Greusel for his bravery in conducting the regiment before being called away.

Captain Porter C. Olson, Co. F, 36th Illinois Infantry took command of the regiment at Stones River after Major Silas Miller was wounded and captured. Promoted to the rank of lieutenant colonel in February 1863, he was killed in action November 30, 1864, at the Battle of Franklin, Tennessee.
(Rick Baumgartner Collection)

"General Cheatham says that battery must be taken"

Private William J. McDearman, Co. H, 12th Tennessee Infantry

About dawn, the battle opened with the Alabama brigade in our front. The Federals were on a hill in the woods; the Alabamians had to go through an open field to attack. The fighting was terrific for some time and our men had to fall back. They were cut to pieces terribly then we were ordered forward to the edge of the field to lie down by an old hedgerow. The enemy cheered like a lot of little schoolboys. Cheatham gave orders for every man to be ready and at his command "attention," each one rose on his right knee and shot under the smoke of the enemy's guns. Then we were to load and fire as we advanced. At the command, every man was in his place, the enemy advancing downhill. We fired all at once and rose yelling; Cheatham's and Cleburne's men could beat the world on a yell.

When we got to the enemy and fired on them, there was a blue line of dead Yanks across the field. We kept as close as possible to them, firing as we advanced. I saw a large ash tree in the edge of the woods and made for it. When I reached it, I was so nearly exhausted that I could scarcely get my breath. I took a swallow of water and then reloaded my gun. Soon, the Yanks battery at our front in the woods opened on us with grape and canister, then their infantry, too. That was a squally time. Our officers hollered 'Charge! Charge! General Cheatham says that battery must be taken if it costs the life of every man." We raised a yell, sent a volley into their lines, started at them, and never stopped until we got the battery of six guns.

The Yankees reformed promptly and charged us. Then orders came thick and fast. "Fire! Fire! Fire, men!" And we did. About that time, 18 guns of the Federal batteries in a cedar brake to our right drove an enfilading fire of canister down our lines and we began to waver. It seemed that every tree and man there would be torn to pieces. The officers got guns and went to work with us, appealing to us to "Stand firm, retreat means death." Soon afterwards I saw our guns, and the wheels of the cannon hardly stopped rolling before our boys opened on the Yankee batteries in the cedar brake. The first round silenced about half of them; every man was quickly in his place and with hat in hand, went yelling like demons.

Private Robert D. Patterson, Co. D, 12th Tennessee Infantry
(Tennessee Confederate Images)

"I became blind, but not unconscious, and fell."

Private James Tingle, Co. B, 93rd Ohio Infantry

In the early morning, we had just completed our breakfast when a

tremendous brisk musket firing began on our right front. At once it began to draw nearer and nearer our vicinity. The Rebels driving our lines back as sheep before the pursuing wolves, for the onslaught of the Rebel force was so heavy and fierce as by mere force of numbers we were driven before in the manner of scared sheep before the destroying wolves. Our right, in confusion, became broken in passing through a heavily timbered spot filled with cedar undergrowth.

Captain Birch with myself and most of Co. B and parts of two or three other companies found on our getting clear of the cedars that our columns were not in sight, but that a line of battle was formed near at hand. Captain Birch organized the men of the 93rd and reported to the colonel of the 19th Ohio who assigned us to his left which then rested on the Murfreesboro Turnpike from Nashville. At this time, it was 11:30 a.m. as I looked at my watch. We were ordered to move slightly to the right in a cotton field. We advanced a few hundred yards in this field and were ordered to lie down where we were. A few minutes later a heavy column of Rebels charged us, and we fell back.

Just at this time, whilst in the act of rising from the ground, a Minie ball struck me when about half arisen from the ground in the right groin. The ball passed under the heavy muscles and flesh, just missing the thigh bone. It came out immediately over the outer hip joint. Private Robert Babbit, being on my left as I occupied the position of first sergeant on the right of the company, asked me if I was hit. I told him yes, but I thought it was not serious. I then placed my right arm over his shoulder, and we started for the rear. When perhaps 50 or 75 yards from the spot where I was first hit, I received a second shot immediately below the right shoulder blade which passed through my body and came out in my breast about one inch above the right nipple. I was at this time just to the right of the pike as you face Murfreesboro. I became blind, but not unconscious, and fell.

*Private Winfield S. Vickers, Co. G, 93rd Ohio Volunteer Infantry
(Rick Baumgartner Collection)*

"The men were true as steel"

Major William F. Douglass, 6th/7th Consolidated Arkansas Infantry

A most destructive fire was opened from the line of infantry and a rifled battery 200 yards immediately in front of my regiment and the action became general on the whole left. In the exposed position occupied by our men our loss just at this point was five times greater than during the rest of the day. About 20 rounds had been fired when the enemy gave way, our men rapidly following past two abandoned guns of the enemy's battery and scores of their dead across the field and into the woods beyond. I may mention here that the advance of McNair's brigade on our left and flanking the enemy was, perhaps, one cause of their giving way on their right, as they had a strong position, and our battery was rendered ineffective by being in our rear on level ground, killing and wounding several of our men while firing over them.

After crossing the fence with my regiment and reaching the position occupied by the enemy's abandoned battery, it was observed that line of the enemy in front of the 5th and 2nd Arkansas Regiments had not given way but still occupied their position behind the fence. Our men were ordered to face obliquely to the rear and deliver an enfilading fire that soon routed them, when the pursuit was maintained by the whole brigade across the wide scope of woods in front to the vicinity of a cotton field and Yankee hospital, where the enemy again made an attempt at a stand, but were rapidly driven back, the right of our regiment passing near the hospital, across the turnpike and into the woods beyond, where we were halted to rest the men and get a fresh supply of ammunition, the firing still being kept up by brigades on our right.

Throughout the entire action our men exhibited the most enthusiastic courage, never flinching from any charge, no matter how desperate, well sustaining that reputation they had won at such cost on other fields. Of the action of the 6th Arkansas Regiment, I need only refer to their long list of killed and wounded to show how gallantly they had acted throughout that day. The 7th Arkansas Regiment was not behind in gallant deeds, those remaining were as true as steel.

The soldiers of General St. John Liddell's all Arkansas brigade suffered heavy casualties driving Colonel Philemon Baldwin's Federals out of their strong position near the Jenkins' woodlot on the morning of December 31, 1862. Among the lost was Private William F. Shores of Co. H of the consolidated 6th/7th Arkansas Infantry who was severely wounded in the abdomen and died of the wound January 7, 1863, at Murfreesboro, Tennessee. (Library of Congress)

"Bubbling out his last breaths through the blood"

Second Lt. John Lendrum Mitchell, aide-de-camp
topographical engineer on General Sill's staff

At early dawn on the 31st, from Johnson came the distant rumble of battle.

This quickly deepened to thunder along our immediate front. The enemy, massed in overwhelming numbers, column closed upon column and under cover of their artillery, bore down upon us with determined tread. Above the rattle of musketry rose the roar of cannons. The air seemed alive with whistling missiles. The concentrated fire of three batteries did not shake in the slightest the battle cloud of gray that was soon to envelop us. Our infantry withheld its fire until the Confederates were close at hand. Then it poured in a well-directed volley. This was a warmer reception than the Rebels have been getting that morning; they hesitated a moment, then turned and ran.

At this critical juncture, a general charge was ordered which was bravely responded to. General Sill sent me along the line to aid in the movement. Hurrying back, I came across the brigade adjutant; he had just seen the general's horse galloping to the rear. In our search for Sill, we almost stumbled over his prostrate body. A bullet had penetrated his brain; he had tumbled from his horse without even a friendly arm to ease his fall. He lay unconscious and lone, bubbling out his last breaths through the blood that thickly flowed over his fair face and silky beard. Two stragglers were with difficulty persuaded to aid in taking his body in a blanket to a farmhouse nearby. Thus died a model of martial virtues, the gentle and chivalric Sill. This scene and its dread surroundings horrified me with war.

But I had no time to "chew the cud of bitter fancy." Our troops did not follow far; they returned to their first position. The enemy, on their side, was making ready to renew the attack. By this time, the divisions of Johnson and Davis had been swept away. Our flank was uncovered, our ammunition expended. Colonel Nicholas Greusel, to whom I had reported, withdrew the brigade in good order from the field under a heavy fire. We left our killed, wounded, and a few horseless guns in the hands of the enemy. The tide of battle surged onward towards the center.

Brigadier General Joshua Woodrow Sill, the only Union general killed at the Battle of Stones River, graduated with the West Point class of 1853. A close friend of his division commander General Phil Sheridan, Sill grew increasingly worried about Confederate movements in his front during the night of December 30th and consequently had his brigade in line and ready for battle long before daylight on December 31st. While galloping towards the 36th Illinois around 7:30 a.m., Sill received his mortal wound, the bullet penetrating through his upper lip beneath his left eye.
(Ohio in the War)

"A most perplexing and unfortunate position"
Private Samuel Seay, Co. C, 1st Tennessee Infantry

The bugles for reveille on the morning of the 31st sounded before it was quite light. Scarcely ten minutes seemed to elapse before the rattle of musketry far to our left beckoned the fact that a battle had begun. Cheatham's division in the second line instantly fell into place, the men throwing their knapsacks into piles with involuntary remarks such as "You know what that means…"

The 1st Tennessee Infantry on the right of Maney's brigade soon found itself on the spot occupied by our front line the night before. To our left a Federal brigade occupied an advantageous position on the wooded hill with a wide stretch of open field in their front and left. A Confederate battery promptly unlimbered and directing a number of shells with accurate marksmanship left some of the enemy dead and wounded at each discharge. Nor were we free from such compliments. It was watching the effect of the Confederate shells upon the enemy that I felt a sharp twinge on the fingers of my right hand and looked down to discover that a bullet had shattered my gunstock, taking off half of it between the two lower bands.

We were ordered to move forward followed by the command to right wheel by regiments, closing closely to the right. We soon were at right angles to the position we had occupied at daylight and found ourselves with our left four companies in a brickyard separated from the others by a pond. Immediately in our front was the Manson [Wilkinson] Pike, well fenced on both sides by high rail fences. I was deliberating upon the disadvantage of climbing them under fire when within less than 200 yards of us came a volley of grape from a battery perfectly masked in a natural cedar brake. Then men in the left wing instantly laid down in the brickyard. The fire with some musketry was simply furious. The position we occupied was one of the most perplexing and unfortunate in which it is possible to conceive a line to be placed. Subjected to a tremendous fire at an exceedingly close range, the direction from which it was fired impressed the minds of the men with the belief that it was own our friends who did the shooting!

Private Sam Watkins of Co. H, 1ˢᵗ Tennessee Infantry suffered his first wound of the war while charging Colonel George Roberts's Illinois brigade near the Wilkinson Pike on the morning of December 31, 1862. "The crest occupied by the enemy was belching loud with fire and smoke and the Rebels were falling like leaves of autumn in a hurricane," he wrote. "I continued to load and shoot until a fragment of a shell struck me on the arm and then a Minie ball passed through the same, paralyzing my arm, wounding, and disabling me." (Company Aytch)

"We could have driven them to the Gulf!"

Private Thomas J. Maxwell, Co. C, 42nd Illinois Infantry

We lay in line in a cornfield one mile from General Rosecrans. The thunders of cannon roused us; after roasting some beefsteak and sweet potatoes which we had the good fortune to capture, we were soon ready and eager for the fray. Johnson's division was surprised on the right and completely routed. The 88th Illinois fought well but was driven back by Cheatham's division.

We were ordered forward to a charge. The enemy were in an open field and we could see them plainly. We fixed bayonets and swept on at a double quick across a cotton field. We ran over the 88th which laid down to let us pass. The Rebels lay down on a slight rise in a stubble field but when we came within about 30 rods of them, they broke and ran like a flock of frightened sheep. Seeing they were making the best time, we sent a shower of bullets after them which halted many.

We kept on half a mile, loading and firing as we ran. The dead and dying strewed the ground such that we had to leap over them. The butternuts pushed up on the left and we had to get out as fast as we got in, but in good order and formed near the batteries. On they came seven columns deep. Now the battle raged and we fought at close quarters sometimes less than ten rods distant. The artillery mowed them down but on they came and we fell back nearly a mile but marked the way with the bodies of the enemy as well as with comrades.

Do not think that we did not do our part. I know that we fought five to one and could that number in front, but when they gave way on both flanks, it is rather more than we profess to be able to stand. The 42nd routed a brigade in the morning and could have driven them into the Gulf if others had done their part. We made three charges through the day and drove them every time. Our brave Colonel George Roberts was killed while rallying to a charge. He has been commanding the brigade nearly a year and had just received a commission as a brigadier.

Captain Wesley P. Andrus, Co. H, 42nd Illinois Infantry
(Allen Cebula Collection)

"Our battle flag was riddled and shot from the staff"

Lt. C. Irvine Walker, assistant adjutant general on staff of Colonel Arthur M. Manigault

General Maney brought up a battery near the gin house to open on the Federal batteries, drawing their attention and ordered Colonel Manigault to charge it with two regiments; he naturally selected his two South Carolina regiments. The 10th South Carolina was brought to the front and supported by the 19th South Carolina we started to advance. While this was going on, General Maney, commanding a Tennessee brigade, moved and formed on the left of Manigault's brigade. Colonel Manigault sent me to General Maney to request him to make a demonstration to aid Manigault's attack as he did not believe the battery was unsupported as he was informed.

As soon as I heard the rattle of musketry from the charge, I galloped back and found the two South Carolina regiments had got into a hornet's nest. The battery being supported by a heavy infantry force. I immediately ordered up the Alabama regiments of the brigade and they reached the South Carolina regiments. Just as the movements of Patton Anderson's brigade on our right had aided us and the whole brigade swept victoriously over the battery. These gallant regiments moved steadily forward and when they reached the enemy's line of skirmishers they charged with a shout, driving the brigade of enemy infantry from the position and silenced every gun of the battery but one. The second line of the enemy appearing in front and a regiment moving around our left flank to enfilade us, they were brought to a stand.

The rest of the brigade was ordered to their support, but this proved inefficient to withstand the numbers of the enemy and as the brigades on our right and left did not move up in time to support ours as had been promised, we were compelled to fall back. Just as we gave way, Anderson's brigade on our right came up but too late to support us. However, they advanced and drove back the enemy, compelling them to leave their battery and take flight. In the charge on the battery the 10th South Carolina lost 85 men, nearly a quarter of the number on the field. Our battle flag was riddled, the blue state flag (Mrs. Wilson's) was shot off the staff but was brought from the field in safety.

First Lieutenant John Robert Ellis, Co. I, 19th South Carolina Infantry
(Liljenquist Collection)

"Our orders were to hold the position at all hazards"

Captain Charles Houghtaling, Battery C, 1st Illinois Light Artillery

On the morning of the 31st, according to orders, we fell back toward the left, or rather changed front to the west, and my battery was placed in a belt of thick timber south of the pike, and was soon hotly engaged with the enemy's batteries, which cut us up severely.

While the battle was raging, I called upon you for reinforcements, which were promptly furnished. Being still unable to silence the Rebel guns, and another battery being opened on me from the left, and being flanked by Rebel infantry, I informed Colonel George Roberts that unless I moved from that position, I should lose my battery, as my horses were falling at every volley, and my men nearly half killed and wounded.

He informed me a few minutes afterward that General Sheridan's orders were to hold that position at all hazards, and I did so until my ammunition was nearly expended, when I was ordered to change front and fire to the left, falling back across the pike, which I did, and three of the guns, being out of ammunition, were sent to the rear, while the others took a position and used the last round of canister on the enemy. Here the remainder of my horses were killed, and being flanked both on the right and left, and no possible chance to get the guns off by hand through the heavy cedar timber in the rear, I was forced to abandon them. All was done that could be, under the circumstances, to save them.

Thus closed the part my company, as a company, took in the engagement. Lieutenant Wright, with some of the boys, joined another battery; Lieutenant Van Dyke and some more fell in with and joined the 26th Pennsylvania Battery, Lieutenant Stevens commanding; some found the Board of Trade Battery, and others took muskets and fell into the ranks as infantry.

We had a terrible fight at Murfreesboro. My battery was lost and I am wounded. My company lost 45 men and 95 horses.

Captain Charles Houghtaling, Battery C, 1ˢᵗ Illinois Volunteer Light Artillery was wounded during the fight for the Wilkinson Pike and "was carried away barely alive, the blood as it flowed from his wound leaving a track on the stones."
(Author's Collection)

"Most of the horses were disabled"

Maj. Gen. Benjamin F. Cheatham

At about 8 o'clock, Colonel Manigault's brigade moved out and attacked the enemy directly in his front. He met with very strong resistance, and after Colonel Loomis was compelled to fall back, and the enemy's fire turned upon his left flank, enfilading his lines, he was compelled to retire. He, however, soon rallied his command, made another gallant attack, and was forced to fall back a second time. At this juncture General Maney's brigade came up and took position on the left of Manigault's, when they moved forward and took position facing toward the Wilkinson pike, near the Harding house, when two batteries of the enemy opened upon them, one of them in the woods on Manigault's right, and on the west side of the Wilkinson pike; the other on east side of the pike.

At this place I came up with Colonel Vaughan's brigade. General Maney had placed Captain Turner's battery of Napoleon guns in position near the brick-kiln, which in a short time silenced the battery on the east side of the road. Colonel Manigault assailed the one in the woods with two regiments, but did not succeed in capturing it. Having made my dispositions, I ordered Colonel Vaughan to move forward with his brigade, and take position on General Cleburne's right, which was in the woods to my front and left. I accompanied General Maney and Colonel Manigault across the Wilkinson Pike, just in front of the enemy's battery last mentioned, which the enemy had abandoned on our approach. The one in the woods to our right was also abandoned, most of the horses having been so disabled that the guns could not be removed.

After crossing the Wilkinson pike, I rode forward to the cedar brake toward the Nashville pike, where I found General Stewart's brigade, hotly engaging the enemy. He captured three of his guns, drove him through the woods and beyond the field to the Nashville pike. During this encounter, Colonel Bratton, of the 24th Tennessee Volunteers, a most gallant officer, was killed. Although my division was originally placed in the second line as a supporting force, it was not long before it was all under fire and hotly engaged with the enemy, and I am proud to say that each brigade did good service. I cannot omit this opportunity to express my thanks for the fortitude with which they bore the hardships and their gallant, soldier-like bearing during the eight trying days they were in line of battle, and most of the time under fire.

Major General Benjamin Franklin Cheatham
(Library of Congress)

"The glug-glug of sharpshooters' balls was incessant"

Sergeant Launcelot Scott, Co. G, 18th Ohio Infantry

Sheridan's division having been driven back, one of his batteries galloped over and took position in our front and commenced shelling some Rebels near a brick kiln. The fire drew a reply from a Rebel battery on our right. The regiment was standing close column en masse. The shells all came over us. Presently one came that just missed. We all ducked our heads. "Good morning!" cried Colonel Josiah Given. "What are you all bowing to me for?" He then put us through the manual of arms and that gave us confidence in ourselves. I don't believe I felt anything like fear after this.

The battle was roaring all around us and still we were standing there. We advanced to within 30 yards of the pike and laid down and awaited the onset of the Rebels. It soon came. Their line marched up with practiced step and the air of veterans. The regiment in our front wore large felt hats. When they arrived near the pike, Colonel Given commanded us to fire and we did with vengeance. We continued firing for about 20 minutes then ceased. Only an occasional shot whistled amongst us now. The regiment that marched up so gallantly was nowhere to be seen. A piece of Sheridan's artillery stood before the left of the company. The near tongue horse was shot the first fire. I laid down behind him and fired. Presently, the other horse received a ball and commenced plunging. He fell and balanced on the tongue. I lay ready to spring if he should roll toward me. Fortunately, he turned the other way and died, his blood pouring on a dead cannoneer.

The Rebels advanced again. A shell came over and struck a tree which fell and killed several men. The charge was not made for the Rebels in our front ceased to fire save for the sharpshooters. We changed front so as to face to the right where Sheridan's division had been. In our front now there was a large open field and we could see regiment after regiment of Rebels marching across and obliquing in behind us. It was not a gratifying sight and our situation became critical in the extreme. The "glug glug" of the sharpshooters' balls was incessant and the tops of the trees threatened to fall on us every instant from the cannon balls that tore through them. It was a curious scene to see the treetops falling without any visible cause. Soon a roar rose in our rear that exceeded anything before heard. The enemy had encountered opposition in their project of surrounding us. The first line was repulsed and we at last received orders to retire from our now worthless position. We retreated several hundred yards and took a position in the cedars about 50 yards in the rear of the first line in the near position.

Sergeant Launcelot L. Scott, Co. G, 18th Ohio Infantry
(Larry M. Strayer Collection)

"We took a battery and stand of colors"

Captain Andrew J. Jones, Co. C, 27th Mississippi Infantry

On the morning of the 31st, the regiment having been in line of battle three days and nights, was ordered forward by Lieutenant Colonel James L. Autry then commanding. We advanced promptly and in good order under a heavy enfilading fire from the enemy's batteries for 300-400 yards when, it being discovered that we were entirely unsupported, we were ordered back to our former position. In a few minutes we were again ordered forward, the regiment moving with the same promptness as our gallant commander displayed great coolness and judgment. This movement was continued through an open field for about 1,000 yards during which time the regiment was thrown upon the left of Chalmers' brigade.

Upon leaving the field, we entered a thick cedar wood where we found the enemy posted in large force. A fierce engagement ensued and here the ever-to-be-lamented hero of Vicksburg, Lieutenant Colonel Autry, gave up his life after ordering the men to lie down while he remained standing, directing them where the enemy was. He had ordered us to take a battery which was pouring a murderous fire into our ranks then was struck by a rifle ball and instantly killed near the battery near a log house, occupied by a company of the enemy who fired upon us through openings. We charged them and the whole party, 35-40 men including the officers, was captured. Simultaneously, the battery and a stand of colors were taken along with a wagon and team, an ambulance, mules, harness, etc.

We still pressed forward commanded by Captain Edward R. Neilson of Co. D, pursuing the enemy through the woods and driving them from their strongholds, killed and capturing many in their flight. About half a mile from where the battery was taken, we came upon the enemy strongly posted. We drove him before us, capturing a number of prisoners and another stand of colors. From there we followed them into an enclosed wood where they seemed to be collecting a large force. Here the fighting was severe. We drove them from the woods into the open field and during the charge Lieutenant M.C. Edwards, commanding Co. E, while charging and encouraging his men was killed.

Private James Monroe Fear of Co. K, 27th Mississippi survived his regiment's charge against the cedars, living long enough to see his grandson Arch Fear go off to war in WWI.
(Library of Congress)

"Colonel Miller cut his way out"

Ordnance Sgt. Adoniram Judson Hastings, 78th Pennsylvania Infantry

Early on the 31st, the enemy massed his forces on the left and fell upon our right under McCook, driving him back in confusion on the center. At 8:40 a.m., I saw Rousseau's troops passing on the double quick to reinforce McCook. The 78th Pennsylvania I found fighting against eight ranks deep of Rebels. Two of these divisions came swooping down on a bayonet charge and surrounded our brigade, but Colonel John F. Miller made a desperate charge and cut his way out, thus saving his command. Our ammunition wagons were entangled among the cedars and there was much confusion- some of our men became panic stricken.

The Rebels pressed on though slaughtered by the scores. The 18th and 19th U.S. Regulars arose as our exhausted brigade retired and poured into the ranks of the enemy a volley which opened gaps, like footprints of the destroying angel. Our General Negley was almost alone at times and stood bravely by his men; he cried when our brigade came out of the trap. Our division was then ordered to support a battery on the left when a masked battery in an orchard opened on us. But ten of our batteries made short work of it and of the half-drunk fiendish Rebels. I say not that they were wounded; they were torn, cut in twain, shattered, beheaded, and disemboweled. Thus, we stood from 2 p.m. to 6:30 p.m. when night closed and we held all the ground except the cedar grove. I walked back on the pike.

Unidentified soldiers of the 78th Pennsylvania pose atop Lookout Mountain in early 1864.
(Liljenquist Collection)

"*Our advance was rapid and fire destructive*"

Brig. Gen. Alexander P. Stewart, commanding Stewart's brigade

After advancing some distance directly to the front across the open field,

the brigade was moved to the left by the flank, so as to place the entire line under cover of the forest from the enemy's artillery fire. The line of infantry advanced through the woods, gradually wheeling to the right, and occasionally halting to readjust the line, and maintaining its supporting distance from Anderson. We shortly arrived at the stone wall built by Anderson's men, where they were placed in line on Sunday, the 28th. Several men were wounded here by the fire of the battery in front.

While in this position the 29th and 30th Regiments Mississippi Volunteers (belonging, as was supposed, to Anderson's brigade) fell back in disorder, leaving a large number of dead and wounded in the open ground beyond the Wilkinson pike, over which they had charged. The brigade moved on from this position to the pike, where it was faced by the left flank and marched a short distance down the road, to bring its right under cover of the woods, when it moved again to the front. It crossed the open ground intervening between the pike and the cedar forest beyond, and advanced to the relief of the front line, which was giving way, and by a rapid fire, commencing with Walker's regiment (the 19th) on the left and gradually extending to the right, repulsed the enemy, who fled in confusion to the dense cedar woods, leaving many dead and wounded behind.

Near the edge of the woods we came upon the battery (1st Missouri) that had previously annoyed us so much, and which the enemy were now attempting to remove. Our advance was so rapid and fire so destructive that they were compelled to abandon two pieces and one or two caissons. We left them behind, and, pressing rapidly forward, drove the enemy before us. They attempted to make a stand at several points, but, unable to endure our fire, were driven through the forest and across the open field beyond to the high ground in the vicinity of the railroad.

*Private L.A. Morphis, Co. F, 5th Tennessee Infantry served in General Alexander P.
Stewart's brigade at Stones River.
(Tennessee Confederate Images)*

"Our position was one of great peril and danger"
Colonel Thomas D. Sedgewick, 2nd Kentucky Infantry (U.S.)

The enemy commenced emerging in heavy force from the woods in our front and on the right, and advanced in column, driving my skirmishers back to the front line. They moved forward in splendid style until they reached the crest of the first hill in our front there halted and delivered a well-directed volley full upon us. Captain Standart's battery immediately on my right and my two regiments in front, simultaneously opened upon them, and with such effect that their front line gave way and fled to the rear; another line was forced up to the same position only to share the same fate; again fresh troops were advanced to the same point in the most perfect order. They planted their colors in the ground and then extended their line by deploying to the right and left. The entire line threw themselves upon the ground and at once opened upon us and kept up a murderous fire.

I discovered that General Negley's entire line had apparently given way, and his troops, artillery and infantry, were then hurrying through the woods in our rear to some point on the left, thus leaving our entire right flank open and unprotected. Our position at this moment was one of great peril and danger. The enemy having driven back to brigade on our left and gained possession of the high grounds around the burnt house, had there posted a battery, one section of which was turned on our position, hurling with fearful accuracy perfect showers of grape and shell. On the right they had pressed closely upon the retiring forces of General Negley and had gained a point within 150 yards of our position, when Captain Standart, wheeling one section of his battery to the right opened upon them with such effect that they were checked, but immediately opened upon our position a terrible fire of musketry.

Meanwhile their batteries and infantry in our front kept up an incessant firing. Thus, we were completely exposed to an enfilading fire of artillery, and musketry, rendering our position untenable, and our capture or annihilation almost certain if we remained. The men, however, stood up nobly, preventing several different attempts to gain our position from the front.

Private Amos Hussey, Co. F, 2nd Kentucky Infantry (U.S.) survived the fight at Stones River unscathed only to be wounded nine months later at Chickamauga. (Liljenquist Collection)

"With a yell such as only Mississippians can give"

Captain Simon Mayer, 10th Mississippi, volunteer aide on the staff of Brig. Gen. James R. Chalmers

Our brigade, with its right resting on Stones River and its left on the Nashville Pike, lay in an open field under cover of the brow of a hill and was formed in echelon. When the order to charge was given, with a yell such as only Mississippians can give, they went over the hill and through the cornfield in front, pouring a murderous fire into the ranks of the enemy and steadily driving them before them. Notwithstanding the showers of shell and grapeshot and the leaden hail of bullets, they went onward until they reached Cowan's house where they were halted and again formed in line. Well might it be said, "In arms, the noble phalanx stood, a living wall, a human hood."

General Chalmers was wounded near Cowan's house by a piece of shell striking him back of the head. The wound is slight but painful; none of his staff officers were hurt. I was thrown from my horse in the early part of the action. He became frightened when a shell burst some 20 feet behind me; he pitched and reared and off I went, nearly breaking my arm but luckily no bones broken. I left the field with General Chalmers and conveyed him to Murfreesboro where he remained at the house of Dr. R.S. Wendell and I remained with him.

This photograph showing members of Co. B of the 9th Mississippi Infantry was taken in April 1861 at Fort Barrancas on the Florida gulf coast by New Orleans photographer J.D. Edwards. Most of the men have been identified from left to right: James Peques, Kinloch Falconer, John P. Fennel, James Cunningham, Thomas W. Falconer (sitting reading a newspaper), James Sims, and John T. Smith. The man standing arms akimbo behind Thomas Falconer has not been identified.

Private Thomas B. Beall, Co. I, 10th Mississippi Infantry wearing a pre-war militia uniform. (Liljenquist Collection)

"We fired a terrible volley as we arrived on the ground"
Private Almon Stuart, Co. I, 9th Indiana Infantry

Wednesday's sun arose bright and beautiful to look down on a scene of carnage, a long day of conflict. Yet ere his beams illumed the east, just at the dawn of day, the cannons' roar proclaimed death's feast and called us to the fray. Our brigade marched out of the woods in which we had passed the night and formed in order of battle in a large cotton field (the cotton was still hanging on the stalk and whitening the ground) with the 41st Ohio and 110th Illinois in the advance. The morning was cold; all of us were flag enough to hover over and around fires, which were burning and smoking in every direction. From early dawn, we had heard heavy firing on our right. As the day advanced, firing was heard on our left and front and soon it seemed as if the enemy were surrounding us.

It was now between 8 and 9 a.m. The 41st and 110th were fiercely engaged with the enemy on our left and front only about a quarter of a mile off. We were at the time ordered to lay down close by the woods that skirted the cotton field. While laying there, a small scale from a stone that had been struck by a shell hit me on my right hand, on the back of it, just drawing blood. (It is now entirely well.) A little before 10 a.m., we formed in line of battle and relieved the 41st. At this time, we could see the fire from the Rebels' guns, both in our front and rear. In our rear, our men were broken, many of them flying in confusion, but we soon forgot them in the conflict in which we now engaged.

We fired a terrible volley as we arrived on the ground the 41st had occupied and three such lusty cheers or yells as we then sent up, heard above the roar of battle and the groans of the wounded. We then lay down or kneeled down on one knee and thus loaded and fired as fast as possible. I stood up almost every time that I fired. Cos. D and I opened to the right and left, making an open space, through which two cannons, stationed a few rods in our rear, belched forth their iron messengers of death. Thus, for hours we fought, with the dead and wounded falling around us. At length, when loading my gun for the 52nd time, a ball from the foe on a death mission bound did its mission forego and dealt me a slight wound on my left index finger. The ball hit me I found, so finding it useless to linger, I in haste left the ground.

Sergeant (later lieutenant) Horace Marble, Co. E, 9th Indiana Infantry
(Liljenquist Collection)

"We advanced under a perfect hail of shot, shell, and grape"
Lieutenant Colonel John H. Anderson, 8th Tennessee Infantry

At about 10 o'clock our brigade was ordered forward. The 8th moved off promptly at the command, under a very heavy cannonade of shot and shell. When we arrived at the position formerly occupied by General Chalmers' brigade, we were ordered to halt and lie down behind the little fortification constructed by his brigade of logs and rails. We remained in this position for about twenty minutes under a perfect storm of shot and shell, causing considerable mortality in my regiment. It soon became apparent to everyone that Chalmers' brigade was giving way, for it was with great difficulty that I could keep his men from running over my men; they came running back in squads and companies.

We were then ordered forward to the charge, which was responded to by the 8th Regiment with a yell, the gallant Colonel William Moore leading. We moved forward at a double-quick, under a perfect hail of shot, shell, and grape, when we arrived at the burnt brick house. The regiment was thrown into some confusion, caused by the house and some picket fence and a portion of Chalmers' men that had remained behind the house, there being several fences and the house and a portion of Chalmers' men that were in the way, causing some four of the companies on the right of the regiment to pass around and through the best way they could.

At this juncture the enemy in our front opened a terrible fire upon us with small arms, at a distance of about 75 or 100 yards. Such a fire I do not suppose men were ever before subjected to. Seeing the condition in which the regiment was placed, with a powerful enemy in our front and on the right and left-for at this time we were then in front of the balance of the brigade, and the enemy were cross-firing me right a left-and seeing so many of my men falling around me, I ordered them forward at a double-quick with fixed bayonets. The gallant 8th responded with a shout and leaped forward like men bent on conquering or dying in the attempt. The enemy in our front contested stubbornly, and those on our right and left continued to pour a deadly fire into us. The enemy's first line gave way before my men; their second was brought forward, but could not stand the impetuosity of our charge, and they gave way.

Colonel William L. Moore of the 8th Tennessee Infantry was killed in action while leading his regiment in its desperate attack against Cruft's and Hazen's brigades near the Cowan Burnt House on the morning of December 31, 1862.
(Find-A-Grave)

"The arrival of General Rosecrans saved us from rout"

Sergeant Henry Breidenthal, Co. A, 3rd Ohio Infantry

On Wednesday morning, our brigade was ordered forward to the right center where we were assigned a position near a dense cedar thicket at about 10 a.m. We were ordered to the right of our division on the double quick and took position on a rising piece of ground amid a dense growth of cedars and threw out skirmishers while we laid down and awaiting the Rebel approach.

We did not have to wait long, however, for the skirmishers on each side soon became engaged. Ours for a time got the advantage and pressed the Rebels sharply for some time, but the enemy, reinforcing their sharpshooters, caused ours to fall back to their former position as the Rebel forces pushed forward regardless of the fire from our men. They kept on moving upon our right flank while the 42nd Indiana poured into them volley after volley. Colonel Beatty perceived the enemy's object being to turn our flank and took precaution to circumvent it by changing front, but still the enemy continued on in the same direction, compelling us to fall back by several movements until we came to an open field fronting the pike.

We remained there but a short time when we were ordered into a new position on the left, facing the enemy's front in the above-named cedar grove. We formed in line, threw out skirmishers, and laid down, keeping up a lively fire upon the enemy's skirmishers who were posted in large numbers behind rocks and trees, harassing us with a galling fire. It was while here that we sustained our greatest loss in killed and wounded. We did not remain here long unsupported but were ordered to gall back which we accomplished in tolerably good order until we came to the open field. There, in the act of forming our regiment in line, another regiment rushed through our partially shattered column, throwing us into considerable confusion. Our major and company officers were all that were left to us, and through their exertions and the opportune arrival of General Rosecrans and part of his staff saved us from total rout.

*Private Owen E. Moore, Co. B, 3rd Ohio Infantry was killed in action at Stones River
(Larry M. Strayer Collection)*

"A volley at short range literally cut them down"

Private Lycurgus Ashbrook Sallee, Co. C, 1st Arkansas Infantry

Our line moved up and after crossing the Wilkinson Pike entered a deep draw parallel to the Nashville Pike when the 15th Kentucky regiment suddenly appeared over a sharp ridge in front of our regiment, the 1st Arkansas. They were at short range and a volley from our regiment literally cut them down, killing their colonel. Soon after, our Major Don McGregor was shot in the thigh and soon died. While in this draw and pressing forward in a dense cedar brake we were under an awful fire of artillery, all the shots passing over our lines save two.

By this time, we were moving slowly but pressing into a dense cedar brake. Brother George was by my side and I noticed we were getting ahead of the line; I feared we would reach the enemy's skirmish line and did. George was in a slight opening when my feet caught some fine vines that threw me and before I could recover, George had pressed through the dense cedars and between two skirmishers. He shot the one on his left and was loading and capping his gun when the second skirmisher ten feet to his right pushed his gun through the cedar and shot George, the ball entering the right side of his abdomen and lodging against the left hip. I went up to him as he fell and said, "George, I was afraid of it."

As I stood talking to him and he to me, a shower of bullets came from the main line 60-70 yards aways in an open field. I pulled George around and sheltered us both as much as I could by a small gum tree until the volley was over. I said to George, "I'll be back directly" and rushed out to the edge of the field and found the enemy line of battle at about face and moving off at common time in good order. I fired on the Yankees until they were 150-200 yards away then went back to George and got him on my back and passed to the rear of the line. I crossed the draw and struck the Wilkinson Pike at a grade in the hillside and had to pass to my left for less grade to cross with my brother. Just above the grade, I found four men sitting "played out" when a most terrific cannonade opened up. A shell struck in the midst of those four men and killed three of them. I turned with my brother on my back to look and saw them sprawled out in all directions and groaning piteously.

Brigadier General Lucius E. Polk
(Liljenquist Collection)

"Scarcely a man came out without the marks of a bullet"

Sergeant Frank Reed, Co. H, 1st Battalion, 15th U.S. Infantry

After pushing forward about a half mile and about 300 yards into a thick cedar swamp, our brigade deployed in line of battle. But scarcely had the movement been executed till it was discovered that we were vastly outnumbered and there were no troops immediately on our left, we were soon flanked and orders were given to fall back. Unfortunately for us, we had to climb a very large cedar fence and before we reached it, Capt. J. Bowmen Bell of the 15th Infantry fell and, in a few moments, expired. In crossing this fence, the battalion was thrown into confusion. Officers became separated from their men, and the men not seeing their leaders, became more and more perplexed, and by the time they could get a few of their men together, the Confederates were so close to us that they were compelled to fire and fall back.

We kept falling back, showing some resistance, until we came to the edge of the woods, where upon our left, the 6th Ohio Infantry had taken position and made a terrible resistance, losing great numbers of their brave fellows; but soon they gave way and now came the slaughter. We had to fall back at least 400 yards through an open field, exposed to the fire of the enemy who had now gained the edge of the woods; and indeed if it had not for our artillery, and had the enemy followed up on the advantage, the result might have been serious in the extreme, but as it was, they soon fell back into the thick timber. For a few minutes the musketry almost ceased, but the artillery still belched forth its smoke and iron hail with a deafening sound which made the very earth tremble. While this was going on, the scattered ranks were again in line and marched forwards to the skirts of the woods ready again for another mortal conflict; but ere our brigade was fairly in position, the volunteers who were on our right gave way, as we had done before, being forced to yield the ground on account of vastly superior numbers. At this fearful crisis, our Major John H. King ordered an advance. We had gone but four or five rods when the enemy again came towering down upon us like the rolling thunder of heaven, engulfing us on the right and in front-making an attempt at extrication, almost certain death; and so, it proved to be, for scarcely a man came out without having been wounded or having the marks of a bullet in his clothing.

Captain Jacob Bowman Bell, Co. D, 1ˢᵗ Battalion, 15ᵗʰ U.S. Infantry was killed during the fight in the cedars at Stones River.
(Find-A-Grave)

"The revolver was used to deadly effect"

Brig. Gen. John A. Wharton, commanding Wharton's brigade

The enemy's immense wagon trains guarded by a heavy force of cavalry, could be seen moving near and in the rear of the enemy in the direction of the Nashville pike. I determined to move across the country, give the cavalry battle, and to attempt to capture the train. Our infantry by this time had succeeded in driving the enemy across the Wilkinson pike. In reaching a point about three-quarters of a mile distant from the Nashville pike, I discovered the wagon train of the enemy, together with some artillery, moving along the pike.

A heavy body of cavalry was drawn up near and parallel to the pike, facing me, and a considerable body was drawn up nearer me to give battle. The battery was placed in position. Ashby's regiment (2nd Tennessee Cavalry) and L.T. Hardy's company formed in front of the enemy. Harrison's command formed on his right flank. The battery opened with considerable effect. It was ordered to cease firing and Ashby and Hardy ordered to charge, which they promptly did. They were met by a countercharge of the enemy, supposed to be the 4th U.S. Regulars, with drawn sabers. At the same time Harrison's command was ordered to charge, which they did in the most gallant and handsome manner. The Rangers, in advance, met the enemy, and completely routed them, relieving Ashby's command, which was hard pressed.

Availing myself of the confusion caused by the rout of the enemy's advanced cavalry, the entire brigade was ordered to charge the enemy's whole cavalry force, drawn up in line half a mile in rear of their main line of battle, protecting their wagon train. The order was responded to in the most chivalrous manner, and 2,000 horsemen were hurled on the foe. The ground was exceedingly favorable for cavalry operations, and after a short hand-to-hand conflict, in which the revolver was used with deadly effect, the enemy fled from the field in the widest confusion and dismay, and were pursued to Overall's Creek, a distance of 2 miles. After they had crossed Overall's Creek, the enemy reformed out of range of our guns.

Private Ed Landvoigt, Co. I, 1st Confederate Cavalry sits at the center with two unidentified comrades.
(Liljenquist Collection)

"The colonel acted without proper discretion"

Captain Martin Buck, Co. H, 1st Ohio Cavalry

Several lines of infantry came charging and cheering right toward us. But on we go in perfect order with skirmishers out in rear to keep them in check as much as possible, and their artillery continuing to drop very often among us, but without doing much damage except to horseflesh. By this time, there began to be evident signs of a regular stampede which, if not checked, which I have no doubt our Colonel saw, and therefore ordered the 1st Ohio to charge without orders from anyone else.

We were yet moving at a rapid pace when the command was given, "Fours left about-draw saber," which was responded to unanimously and in good order while not more than 100 yards from us was a long line of Rebel cavalry popping away at us as though they didn't care if they hit somebody. But now the command "Charge" was given, and the boys went in with a yell, the Colonel leading. After charging and driving their first line several hundred yards, we came to another line to our right, drawn up at nearly right angles, which gave us a crossfire as we passed them, but being on rather lower ground than they were, I think they must have shot over us, particularly Co. H as we were on the right and nearest to them. They now began to close in around us when all saw at a glance that we had to cut our way out or be taken prisoners, so all, except those who had already surrendered, now took the chances of being shot in the back rather than surrender as prisoners of war. Your humble servant was among the latter, and by the good use of spurs and pistols, escaped without even a scratch; but I am perfectly satisfied that I had not some bullet holes through me when I had made an examination. In this affair, Colonel Minor Millikin and Lieutenant Condit and two privates were killed; Lieutenant Scott and several privates were wounded and 40 or 50 taken prisoners. The Colonel, overanxious to distinguish himself in this war, probably acted in this affair without proper discretion, but he was nevertheless a brave man and exhibited more coolness and presence of mind than any other cavalry commander on the ground.

Colonel John Minor Millikin of the 1st Ohio Cavalry was killed in combat with Private John Bowers of Co. K, 8th Texas Cavalry during his regiment's charge along Asbury Lane. (Rick Baumgartner Collection)

"The slaughter seemed greater than any other"
Brig. Gen. Sterling A.M. Wood, commanding Wood's brigade

We passed across the field and through a wood and across the Nolensville pike, driving the enemy. Here we entered another field and became engaged with a heavy force in our front, while a battery of several guns was enfilading our entire line. The ammunition of several guns was enfilading our entire line. The ammunition of several regiments became exhausted, and we returned to the wood for shelter, while we refilled our boxes.

At this place Brigadier General Johnson's brigade came up, and he formed it and marched off to our right. We soon followed, and, by direction of Major General Cleburne, took position on the left of Brigadier General Polk's brigade. The line now marched against the enemy for the third time. He was again posted in a dense cedar brake. From this position our men drove him. At this point the slaughter seemed to be greater than any other. We drove the enemy out of the woods and across a field, under cover of a large number of guns which he had collected at this point. The fire from his artillery became very annoying, and the men took shelter in the timber. By direction of Major General Cleburne, I sent forward about 100 sharpshooters to pick off his horses and cannoneers, but they could not cover themselves from the fire of his whole line of infantry and were forced back to the edge of the field.

About this time Colonel A.J. Vaughan, jr., came up with his brigade, and I directed it into position on my left. It had a sharp contest with the enemy, driving him back. My men, as reported by their colonels, having expended their ammunition, I formed them in rear of the cedar brake and collected parts of several regiments, which had become separated from their commands, to wit, about 100 men of the 45th Alabama, under Lieutenant-Colonel J.G. Gilchrist; about 70 of the 1st Louisiana Infantry, under a captain; a part of a Mississippi regiment of another corps, all of which I conducted to the wood near our ammunition wagons.

First Lieutenant Isaac Croom Madding, Co. B, 16th Alabama Infantry of General S.A.M.
Wood's brigade.
(Liljenquist Collection)

"The regiment suffered most terribly in the fire"
Major Charles Manderson, 19th Ohio Infantry

Defeat seemed imminent. On our hurried way, the 19th Ohio, leading Crittenden's division met horses, teams, and men in confusion most confounded. General Rousseau, riding bare-headed, cries to me, "What troops are these?" To my answer, he said with fearful entreaty in his voice, "For God's sake! Get quickly to the cedars on our right and stop this rout." We hastened on. General Rosecrans, pale with anguish but determined of purpose and confident in bearing, says, "Men! You can save the day. Will you do it?" I said, "Aye, aye, sir! If mortal men can, we will!"

We pass from the march by the flank into line under the direction of the commanding general himself, my regiment forming the right of the front line. The graycoats, flushed with success, came gaily on. We waited until they were within easy range. It is a weary waiting and hard to endure. Our men are falling rapidly under the fire of the advancing foe. My favorite mare drops dead with a ball through her gentle heart. Adjutant Brewer, always alert and devoted, replaces her with his good gray. Rising from the ground with no great bodily harm, I exclaim, "Adjutant, my glasses broken into many bits and I see dimly." He quickly replies, "Never mind, I will see for you" and so he did, gallant fellow. At last, the order to fire! From every musket leaps a missile of death. The Confederate line wavers! Strong young teeth tear the cartridges. We load and fire with energy. The gray line breaks!

A charge is ordered by Rosecrans in person. They run! How inspiring! What exhilaration! With wild yells we rush on. We regain much of the ground lost in the early morning and hold it fast and firm. We were here but a few minutes when our right support gave way and left our regiment greatly exposed to a flanking fire. I sent word twice to Colonel Beatty that the enemy had flanked our position in great force, but received no order. The regiment was suffering most terribly from the fire and, seeing the enemy within 50 yards of our right and in position to destroy us. I ordered a change of front to the right to rear.

Major Charles Manderson led the 19th Ohio Infantry in the fighting along Asbury Road despite losing his spectacles in the fight. The Ohioan survived the battle and ended the war as colonel of the regiment. He later served as senator from Nebraska, this cabinet card dating from his time in Washington, D.C.
(Library of Congress)

"Such was the spirit and vigor of the men"

Colonel Alfred Jefferson Vaughan, commanding brigade

When about half through the woods, engaging the enemy on my right flank as I went along, I met a line of battle somewhat lapping my left, which I found to be Wood's brigade, engaging another force of the enemy in his front. General S. A. M. Wood desired my support to save him from being flanked on the right. Accordingly, I moved forward and engaged this force, driving him across the open field and dirt road into the only remaining field between us and the Nashville pike, where a large wagon train of the enemy was distinctly visible.

At this point I found myself about to be flanked on my right by a strong force of the enemy posted in the woods to the right of the field. Seeing no signs of any support on my right, which I had supposed was following me to continue my alignment on the right, I concluded to rapidly continue my advance upon the enemy, which had been driven toward the pike and which had again rallied, and formed in line, and, by driving him, to force the troops threatening my flank to retire. Such was the spirit and vigor with which my men pursued this object that the troops on my left did not keep up with them, and before I could effect the purpose I had in view, my right flank was so severely enfiladed that I was compelled to retire them after again driving the enemy from one of his batteries, which on that account I was unable to bring off.

Withdrawing my troops to the Wilkinson pike, I there remained in line of battle on our extreme left for the remaining short portion of the day and for the entire night.

Colonel (later General) Alfred J. Vaughan
(Library of Congress)

"Seconds seemed minutes and minutes seemed hours"

First Lt. Marvin Benjamin Butler, Co. A, 44th Indiana Infantry

We moved on the pike about a half mile on the double quick, came to a halt and right front, moved forward in line of battle. First, we moved through a cedar chopping, then into and across an open field perhaps 80-100 rods across, going over quite a high ridge which we parallelled with our line, then down a slope to a high cedar rail fence next to a piece of thick, young timber, clean and clear of undergrowth. This fence was let down in gaps every 15 feet and when ready, all passed through, formed our line and dropped and dropped flat on the ground.

The enemy was in heavy force, 15 rods in front, behind temporary breastworks, hastily built of old logs and the wood on the right was full of Rebel infantry with a battery of artillery. We were already flanked on the right and had hardly touched the ground when the Rebel yell was responded to by a heavy volley of musketry from the front, and canister, grape, and musketry from the right. We were in a slaughter pen and while our line was steady and cool, firing low and as rapidly as possible, it was evident that we could not hold the position many minutes, Very fortunately for us, the enemy's balls flew high, from 3-10 feet over us, or every man in our line would have been killed or wounded. We pressed the ground hard and I am quite sure my impression could have been seen for some time thereafter.

Fred Swambaugh lay close to my right and Luy on his right. How long it was after the engagement began, I'm unable to say, as seconds seemed minutes and minutes seemed hours when Fred was struck by a ball in the back. Nelson ordered Lu and me to take him back. To lie still, we were comparatively safe but to get up seemed certain death. We obeyed the order, however, raised Fred to his feet for his lower limbs were paralyzed. He threw his arms around our necks and we carried him back through the gap and up the slope, three abreast, a splendid target for every Rebel in either line. Their balls struck and tore the gravel on either side, whipped around our feet, legs, and heads, and whistled and pinged close to our ears, harmlessly an invisible omnipotent hand shielded us as we carried our heavy burden up that long hill, to and over the crest out of range where we stopped to get our breath.

Two companies of the 44th Indiana Infantry pose in their encampment in Chattanooga, Tennessee in May of 1864. Known as the "Iron 44th, the Hoosiers took part in the heavy fighting along Asbury Road on December 31st and near McFadden's Ford on January 2nd. Company H is pictured above while Co. G is pictured below. (Library of Congress)

"The engagement was now in the height of grandeur"
Captain William H. Harder, Co. D, 23rd Tennessee Infantry

After advancing for almost a mile, we were ordered to halt and form a regular line by right alignment. Just as our regiment got up into its place, we could see some distance in front through the thick cedars a corps of men that appeared to be Confederates. Sometimes they advanced, then moving towards our left as if desirous of uncovering our line. We were in doubt of who they were. They advanced until within about 100 yards of our line and then with folded colors, laid down amongst the stones and cedars.

Colonel Richard Keeble asked me to go near them and find out who they were. I went down the road towards them; there were many of them in brown clothing and I was taken off guard until within 40 yards. They rose up at me and fired a heavy volley, missing me but killing and wounding 16 men in the road behind the line. I, of course, retired. The firing opened with great fury and drove our whole brigade over the crest of the hill. I called to our regiment and returned to the line under a galling fire. The brigade all came in line and then broke again.

Our regiment remained in place pouring volley after volley down the road and received volleys in return. The brigade returned to fire a second time. After a half hour of firing, the Federal artillery opened on us and at the first fire the whole line broke in confusion. I seized our regimental colors and remained on the line with no one save the color bearer. The men of the regiment, seeing my maintaining the colors, returned to the line followed in a few minutes by the whole brigade. The engagement was now in the height of grandeur; our regiment poured in a solid fire for almost an hour. The trees were cut down by the artillery and then riddled to splinters by the rifle shots. But then our artillery entered the action and in five minutes the small arms fire ceased. The Federals to our front seemed annihilated.

Private Allen Buckner Pollock, Co. B, 23rd Tennessee Infantry
(Tennessee Confederate Images)

"A scene most terribly exciting"

First Lt. Wilbur F. Hinman, Co. E, 65th Ohio Infantry

As we neared the scene of action, everything was in the wildest confusion.

A short distance ahead was heard the low booming of cannon and the sharp rattle of musketry. Infantry regiment after regiment, batteries of artillery, and squadrons of cavalry were being hurried forward with the utmost possible speed. Hundreds of ammunition and hospital wagons were being pushed out over the stony pike to get them out of the way. Couriers were riding furiously to and fro, officers shouting commands to their men, the shells bursting in every direction, all combined to form a scene most terribly exciting.

Now came the intelligence that a heavy column of the enemy was advancing still farther to our right for the purpose of turning our right flank and it must be checked. If the Rebels were successful in flanking us, the battle was inevitably lost. Our brigade was sent as a kind of forlorn hope to prevent this occurrence. Off we went further and further to the right. At length, the enemy's long line was formed and was discerned advancing to the front; we promptly formed to meet them. We moved forward steadily awaiting with the most intense anxiety the commencement of the conflict. Cos. I and H were deployed as skirmishers and sent ahead under the command of Major Horatio Whitbeck and were soon sharply engaged with the enemy's sharpshooters. The Rebels approached under the cover of the woods while we were in the open field and as we ascended the rise of ground, the skirmishers balls whistled around us pretty lively.

We advanced a short distance into the woods and immediately the action became general. We loaded and fired lying down and the Rebels ditto, the lines being about 200 yards apart. I have often read of battles and formed ideas concerning them but the reality far exceeds anything I ever conceived. Our battery opened with shell and was replied to by a Rebel battery on their left. The roar of artillery and musketry was deafening while every moment it seemed as though a score of balls were hissing as near my head as they could without striking. Many of our gallant boys were soon stretched on the ground killed or wounded and oh, how our hearts ached to hear the groans of the suffering without being able to do anything for their relief!

First Lieutenant Wilbur F. Hinman, Co. E, 65th Ohio Infantry later penned not only a regimental history but the highly regarded book Si Klegg and His Pard.
(Gary Milligan Collection)

"Colonel Murray bore the colors to the front"

Brig. Gen. St. John R. Liddell, commanding Liddell's Brigade

The brigade being now supplied with ammunition, after having crossed the Wilkinson turnpike, was rapidly pushed forward through the woods a quarter of a mile or more, and coming up with the enemy on the edge of a field, which opened in view of a church, in some open woods on Overall's Creek, some 500 yards distant on our left, and engaged him, driving him in confusion over the crest of a hill beyond. Finding myself alone at this point, with no support on my right or left, I halted my command in the woods near the fence and threw forward a line of skirmishers to reconnoiter and develop the enemy, not then visible from our position.

Lieutenants J.M. Dulin and J.L. Bostick, of my staff, who had gone forward with the skirmishers, immediately returned and reported the enemy in line of battle in the valley of Overall's Creek, some 400 or 500 yards distant from the crest of the hill. I at once ordered forward my battery to the crest of the hill, and directed it to fire upon him, as I was in good supporting distance with the brigade. This was done with decided effect, resulting in turning the enemy back and driving him from view behind the railroad embankment.

I then returned with the battery to my command in the woods and moved by the right flank until I got in sight of Brigadier General Johnson's command, which by this time had come up from the Wilkinson road. After rejoining General Johnson's left, I moved forward, and almost immediately engaged the enemy, whose right lay across a neck of woods, the left being behind a fence in front of my right. After a very severe engagement of some twenty minutes, we repulsed him on our right, throwing him into confusion, he still, however, maintaining his ground upon our left, on which we concentrated the fire of the 5th, 6th, and 8th Arkansas Regiments, soon breaking, after a sharp contest, his line at that point also. It was here that Lieutenant-Colonel Murray, of the 5th Arkansas Regiment, took the colors of his regiment and gallantly bore them to the front, encouraging his men to the contest. A beautiful stand of United States colors was captured by Private J.K. Leslie, of his regiment.

Brigadier General St. John Richardson Liddell commanded a brigade at Stones River and left an incredibly detailed memoir of his service with the Army of Tennessee. (Library of Congress)

"Were all the men killed and wounded?"

Captain Frederick Garternicht, Co. G, 84th Illinois Infantry

On the 31st of December we were formed in line of battle; our regiment, which had been in advance of the brigade the last two days was this day in the reserve. About 9 o'clock, the cannonading began and very soon the infantry fire got heavy. We were ordered forward to support a battery and were, for about half an hour, sharply engaged. Here, Lieutenant Mills of Co. K got wounded, and many others of the regiment, but none in my company. We had to change front and took our position in front of a ledge of rocks surrounded by a cedar grove. Here we laid, our artillery firing over our heads. The battle was in its fury. Regiment after regiment on our right and left gave way, some of them in utter confusion. We still stuck in our rocks.

Secesh balls now commenced to tell upon us. The first I noticed as being wounded was Lafayette Crandall. He had been loading and firing when, all at once, he rolled over and cried out, "Captain, I am hurt." I went up to him; he was shot in the neck. I have not heard anything of him since neither have we found him among the dead. On my right a man of Co. K was shot in the ear, behind me was Corporal Green, shot in the face, this all happened inside of 10-15 minutes.

When we were ordered to fall back, we had to go under a heavy fire some 200 paces when we halted again for a short time but not long. We were ordered into a railroad cut; here I wanted to arrange my company again and found Lieutenant Fuller, myself, and only six men present. I thought my men were mixed up with some other company in the regiment, but I could not find another one. Were they all killed and wounded? That could not be! Before the battle, the strength of our regiment was 328 men in all; of these, 159 were killed and wounded while 8 are missing.

*Captain Frederick Garternicht, Co. G, 84th Illinois Infantry
(Scott Bumpus Collection)*

"After a bloody combat the enemy were finally dislodged"
Lt. Gen. William J. Hardee, commanding Hardee's Corps

Cleburne had now driven back all the forces of the enemy beyond the Wilkinson road, when another line was displayed in the cover of the cedar woods between the Wilkinson and Nashville turnpike. Wood, Polk, and Johnson charged this line, receiving a heavy fire. Here Lieutenant Colonel Don McGregor, of the 1st Arkansas, and Major J. T. McReynolds, of the 37th Tennessee, two brave officers, fell, mortally wounded. Brigadier General Liddell attacked the enemy near the left of Brigadier General Johnson, whom he had rejoined, and, after an obstinate conflict, threw them into confusion. Lieutenant Colonel John E. Murray, of the 5th Arkansas, courageously bore the colors of his regiment to the front, while Private J. K. Leslie, of the same regiment, captured the colors of the enemy with his own hands. A portion of Cleburne's division was repulsed, but, after a bloody combat, the enemy were finally dislodged.

On our right their lines remained unbroken. With our inferior numbers no further advance could be hazarded until all my forces were collected. Wood, having fallen back for ammunition, was detained to protect the ordnance train. The remaining brigades occupied the cedar brakes and fields near the Nashville road. The command of Cleburne was now reformed, and about 3 o'clock he essayed to rout a fresh line of the enemy near the Nashville turnpike. The enemy were again broken with heavy loss. Johnson's brigade was conspicuous in the conflict, in which the brigade of Preston Smith also shared.

It was now past 3 o'clock. In moving through the open grounds to drive the enemy from the last positions they held near the railroad, a fierce and destructive enfilading fire of artillery was poured upon the right of Cleburne's division from batteries massed near the railroad embankments. At this critical moment the enemy brought up a fresh line to oppose our weary troops. Our ammunition was exhausted. Smith's brigade recoiled in confusion. Johnson and Polk followed, and the division was repulsed. It was rallied and reformed in the edge of the cedar woods, about 400 yards in rear of the most advanced position we had won.

Lieutenant General William J. Hardee, former commandant at West Point, led a corps for most of his service with the Army of Tennessee and for a brief time after the defeat at Chattanooga in late 1863, held command of the entire army.
(Library of Congress)

"Their shots told fearfully on us"

Captain Henry Haymond, Co. E, 3rd Battalion, 18th U.S. Infantry

Our regiment was ordered immediately about face to support our battery. We got out of the timber and formed on the left of the battery as soon as we could. In a few moments the enemy had cleared our troops out of the extreme right of the cedar woods, and now by a flank movement attempted to capture all those to our left. This could only be done by capturing our battery. They knew it was a fearful thing to attack a battery in an open field but nevertheless they attempted it.

They advanced boldly with columns doubled upon the center, their long grey lines stretching from one side of the field to the other when within fair range the six heavy guns of Guenther's Battery each loaded with 96 cannister shot thundered over the plain. I could distinctly see wide deep gaps cut out of their ranks, but still they advanced. They were playing a deep game but if successful the day was theirs. Two or three more times the battery hurled death into their ranks. No troops in the world could stand such slaughter. They broke and ran in confusion. I saw their battle flag (white ground with a red crop) shot down twice but still some bold spirit bore it aloft. A third time it fell and was not raised again but left upon the field. Foiled in his attempt to take our battery, the enemy turned his attention to the troops upon our left, and in a few moments the face of the country was filled with fugitives from our overpowered army. The fate of the day being upon the balance.

The Regular Brigade as a last resort was then ordered forward to check the enemy's advance until the army could be reorganized. We entered the cedar woods in the line of battle just as the last of McCook's corps was driven out of it. The enemy bore down upon us in three or four lines, their front rank would fire and fall down and load, the rear rank firing over their heads, by this means they poured an incessant fire into us. The 18th U.S. met them gallantly and now commenced one of the most terrific musketry firings that has occurred during the war. They had the advantage of position, and in standing beneath the shadow of the pines enveloped in smoke, while we stood at the edge of the timber in bold relief against the light. They fired very low, and their shot told fearfully upon us.

Captain Henry Haymond, Co. E, 3rd Battalion, 18th U.S. Infantry
(Rick Baumgartner Collection)

"Among the lost was our gallant color bearer"

Captain William A. Cotter, Co. H, 30th Arkansas Infantry

We moved on near a mile in the direction the enemy had retreated, when it was discovered that they had rallied and stood in line of battle in rear of a most powerful battery, which was planted upon a hill commanding the country for some distance on three sides, and which was also supported by two small batteries, holding a crossfire upon any advance by the front.

When we arrived within 500 yards of this battery, the third command to "charge that battery" was given. This, too, was responded to with a joyous shout and a rapid onward. All were fatigued, but all were willing, all were sanguine. But here we were disappointed, for it was here that we met with our first repulse. But it was unavoidable on the part of our brigade, for by the time we had advanced to within 300 yards of the center battery the enemy began to pour in grape at such a murderous rate that it appeared little less than suicide to advance farther. Still, some few, nothing daunted, determined to go on, and some did go to within 100 yards of the enemy's stronghold. Among the rest was our gallant flag-bearer, whose hand was shot off and he was compelled to abandon his colors.

It was under that battery that we sacrificed some of our noblest spirits - first of all, our gallant major, James J. Franklin. Knowing a second attempt upon this stronghold of the enemy to be altogether impracticable, we fell back near 1,200 yards, where we rallied our scattered men and moved forward again about 800 yards. Here we were ordered to remain until nightfall.

Colors of the 30th Arkansas Infantry which were captured after the gunners from Battery H, 5th U.S. Light Artillery pummeled the Arkansans near the Nashville Pike. Major Anson McCook led the detachment of troops from the 2nd Ohio who retrieved these colors along with the battered survivors of the color guard. The flag measures 40 inches on the staff by 46 inches on the fly and calls out two battle honors for Farmington, Mississippi and the Battle of Richmond, Kentucky. By the end of January, this flag was displayed in a store window in Steubenville, Ohio where it was "suspended on a short wooden staff, painted black. The flag is bunting, blue and white. The flag was taken by the brave 2nd Ohio for which the struggle must have been desperate as the flag is pierced with bullets and stained with blood." Interestingly, the 30th Arkansas was re-designated the 25th Arkansas shortly after Stones River and another regiment subsequently was renamed the 30th Arkansas! Eventually, the flag was sent to the War Department in Washington and recorded as flag capture No. 80. The flag was returned to the state of Arkansas in 1906.

"Up boys and let them have it!"

Sergeant Tobias Ross, Co. B, 2nd Ohio Infantry

We had scarcely double quicked into position before the ball opened in the woods we had just left and in a short time regiments came rushing from the woods, in more or less disorder, but none broke until the 15th U.S. Regulars came out in complete disorder and made directly for where we were lying flat on our faces, the Rebels close in their rear and cutting them down at every step. They immediately charged for Loomis' battery, but our colonel shouted, "Up boys and let them have it!" We instantly jumped to our feet and poured a well-directed fire into their close ranks, which brought them to a halt. They were within 100 yards of us, and you may imagine the effect of our fire. I think there was scarcely a ball ineffective. Their color bearer fell at the first fire, and we captured their flag. We would have let them come still nearer, if it had not been for the cowardly Regulars being in our way.

I stood in one place and fired 15 rounds. We then charged and routed them completely. We lost in this charge 35 men- our beloved Colonel Kell and Andy Ward being of the number. I do not wish to brag or boast, but I do certainly think if we had broken and run, the day would have been lost past redemption and the grand Army of the Cumberland would have been this day among the things that were, and in place of a glorious victory, disaster and defeat. Our repulse of the enemy was the first check they had up to this time received and was given under the immediate eyes of Generals Rousseau and Rosecrans.

General Rousseau rode down our line, hat in hand, stopped in front of every company, and warmly thanked them for their gallantry, and said he could depend on the Ninth Brigade. You can imagine the effect of seeing your friends run and desert you in a tight place, but it was still worse for the old 2nd Ohio for our friends ran through our lines, causing more or less confusion for a moment, but the glorious boys closed up instantly without a break. Bitter and fierce were the curses we bestowed on the cowards as they crowded past, but they said nary a word. When the Rebels fell back, our regiment was immediately advanced with Companies A and B being deployed as skirmishers.

*Private Alexander Gaines Walker, Co. I, 2ⁿᵈ Ohio Infantry was killed in action along the
Nashville Pike.
(Find-A-Grave)*

"We fell back in good order under the circumstances"

Colonel Julius A. Andrews, 15th Texas Cavalry (Dismounted)

My regiment continued to advance until we arrived at a rail fence, which was 100 yards from the front of my regiment at the time the enemy opened fire on my skirmishers, and about 40 yards from the hedge of cedars. We soon arrived at the fence and passed over it, at which time I gave the command "charge." My regiment charged, driving the enemy promptly before them out of the hedge. We continued the charge for about 100 yards, which brought us some distance beyond the hedge in an open wood.

The front of my regiment by this time was unmasked by the enemy's infantry, having driven them to our left. A heavy cannonading quickly ensued from masked batteries, stationed about 150 yards distant, and opposite the right of my regiment and the left of the 14th Texas commanded by Colonel J.L. Camp. The fire of shot, shell, and grape being so terrific, I ordered my regiment to stand, which they did. We were at this time under a heavy fire of musketry and artillery, my regiment, in conjunction with Colonel Camp's, having halted and held the enemy in check for about 15 minutes. I at time discovered that the two regiments composing the right of the brigade had been separated, from some unknown cause, from my regiment and Colonel Camp's. I cautioned my regiment to stand fast and continued the fire.

I approached General Matthew D. Ector, who was stationed at the time in the rear of the center of my regiment, cheering my men on. I asked him where the balance of the brigade was. He replied he did not know. I then remarked to him it was impossible for my regiment and Colonel Camp's to contend against a brigade of infantry and the artillery, too, as our regiments were comparatively small. He then remarked, "We had better give back." I then returned to my command and ordered them to five back, the booming of cannon and musketry being so terrific at the time that it was impossible for my voice to be heard only by those who were near me. However, the men who heard the command obeyed it, which was discovered by the men up and down the line; also by the left of Colonel Camp's regiment, which caused both regiments to fall back in as good order as possible, under the circumstances.

Colonel Julius A. Andrews, 15th Texas Cavalry (Dismounted)
(Library of Congress)

"Hold your fire until you see the whites of their eyes!"
Private Charles H. Maple, Chicago Board of Trade Battery

On Wednesday morning we moved from the woods to the open field about a mile and a half from the enemy's front and had gone about 300 yards when zip went a shell just over our heads, then another, then a shot, then two or three together, until the whole air seemed filled with these deadly missiles. We laughed at first, but in a few moments, we were ordered to take a position and it was not long before we sobered down and nary a laugh. The fire increased all the time until the roar was almost deafening. Suddenly a howl was heard from the Rebs, then see a man running out of the woods and presently the firing begins to cease, and as the roar dies away, the howling increases. Soon our right wing was in full retreat and at this juncture our battery is ordered to commence firing with this injunction from Captain Stokes, "Hold your fire, boys, until you see the whites of their eyes and then give it to them!"

For one hour our boys poured in the shell and canister so fast that the forward course of the Rebs was checked. We are now ordered to charge forward and move forward about 200 yards and again commenced to fire; all the time the bullets and shells were showering around us faster than you ever saw hail in Illinois. Just opposite us on a corresponding hill, the Rebs could be plainly seen, every action and movement clear. We had been in this position but a few moments when the Rebs prepared to charge. On they came, a moving forest of bristling bayonets, one of the sublimest, yet most awful sights I ever beheld. Gently they descended the hill on the other side, cross the valley, and ascend the hill on which the battery is stationed.

Now the sight becomes terrifically sublime; round shot after round shot goes screaming through the air or tear their way through the living masses; shell after shell chased each other overhead and bursting in sulfurous canopy scattered their fragments far and wide, dealing out death in every direction. The enemy began to waver, and our boys began to work faster and pour in the shot so fast that they are compelled to fall back, and to the Board of Trade Battery is given the honor of saving the army from a total defeat. After we took our second position, General Rosecrans, who was just behind was just behind the battery cheering and urging the boys.

A detachment of Federal gunners demonstrates how to load a field piece. Federal batteries at Stones River usually consisted of six guns split into sections of two guns, each section under the command of a lieutenant. Sergeants commanded each individual gun crew which consisted of ten men, each assigned specific tasks to ensure efficient loading and discharging of the piece. For example, No. 1, pictured here, uses the sponge to first swab the barrel of any burning residue from the previous shot; once complete, No. 2 shown here holding the shell would place the next powder bag into the barrel which is pushed by No. 1 with the rammer all the way to the breech. Other soldiers would prick open the powder bag, cut fuses, and insert the friction primer. Once all steps were complete, the men would stand clear and the No. 4 pulls the lanyard to fire the weapon. A well-drilled gun crew could discharge their gun around once per minute.
(Liljenquist Collection)

"Be men and strike for vengeance and liberty!"

Captain Ezekiel John Ellis, Co. E, 16th Louisiana Infantry

We crossed the river and were halted not far from the bank. In front, the battle was raging with terrific fury. Over us, pieces of artillery were shaking the hills and the Yankee shells were flying over us. At this moment, General Bragg rode by us. Loud cheers greeted him as he passed rapidly along the line and hastily checked his horse in front of the colors, turned towards us, pulled off his cap and waved it as if for silence. I shall never forget Bragg as I saw him then with his pale emaciated face slightly flushed with the ardor of battle, his fierce eyes, supernaturally large and full of light, his thin lips compressed, and his form compact yet attenuated, so upright and firm in the saddle while he restrained his restive horse.

He waved his cap and all was hushed in an instant. Then the rigid lips unclosed, the stern brow was unbent and the words came short and clear with a force that dared you to forget. "Louisianans," said he. "The enemy's right has been routed and we are steadily driving it back. He still stands firm in the center. He must be defeated there. It remains for you to do this and the victory is ours. Remember the wrongs of your state, your insulted wives and mothers, your polluted shrines, and desecrated homes. Be men and strike for vengeance and for liberty!" The most deafening cheers greeted the general as he rode rapidly away towards where the conflict seemed fiercest. Then we began to advance moving by the right flank. Every heart was full of enthusiasm. Each man seemed to feel that no task was beyond our accomplishment.

We were now moving through a cotton field and the enemy began to shell our line. One shell killed Ed Parmele and Japhet Harull of my company. They were mangled and torn to pieces and died in an instant. The same shell killed Captain Oliver's horse and broke the handle of a litter in the hands of the bearer. It burst right in the ranks and I wonder that more of the men were not injured. As we reached the turnpike the regiment was placed in column right in front. For 200 yards we marched in column up the pike under a fierce artillery fire. Shell and shrapnel hissed and screamed and burst about us, but with steady tramp and arms at the right shoulder shift the column moved swiftly and steadily on.

Private James Nolan Murphy, Co. E, 16th Louisiana Infantry with his wife and young son.
Murphy was killed in action charging the Round Forest near the Nashville Pike.
(Stan Hutson Collection)

"This position must be held"

George H. Woodruff, regimental historian of the 100th Illinois Infantry

The sound of musketry comes nearer. The 100th is in danger of being flanked.

It is ordered to change its position to avoid this new danger. It comes upon another regiment, which proves to be the 110th Illinois. The men exchange cheers as they ascertain that two Illinois regiments are together and feel inspired with new strength and courage. This position must be held, for it is one of great importance. After a little, a regiment in the rear is withdrawn, and the two, 100th and 110th are left alone. They move forward to the edge of a cotton field. The enemy try hard to dislodge them, but here they lie, hugging the earth, while they are treated to a brisk cannonade, and our own batteries are replying over them. What terrific music! The shrieking of shells, the thunder of artillery, the crash in the tree tops overhead; and here thy lie, unable to do aught but hold on - the most trying position in which men can be placed.

But now the order comes to "fall in," and just as they are doing so, a solid shot comes along which takes off the head of Giles L. Greenman, of Co. K, and strikes Lieutenant Worthingham, of the same company, in the breast, killing him instantly. Five poor fellows yielded up their lives at this point, and about 30 were wounded. The regiment is moved across the railroad, when knapsacks are unslung, and it is formed along the railroad. Meanwhile the bullets fly thick and fast, and with telling effect upon the ranks, and one after another of the men limp by to the rear. They lay down on this line.

Soon an American flag was seen in front, and a regiment marched in by the flank, on the south side of the cotton field, and it was, of course, supposed to be one of ours, as they had on U.S. overcoats. But soon the boys saw the "butternut," and gave them a volley. They went over the fence, and down the hill, like a lot of sheep. Lieut. Mitchell, of Wilmington, here receives the wound which proved mortal three days after. The men lie and listen to the grim music of the shot and shell flying over their heads, and cutting the cedars, anxiously waiting for the result on the field at large.

Colonel Frederick A. Bartleson of the 100th Illinois lost an arm at Shiloh, would be captured at Chickamauga, and lose his life at Kennesaw Mountain in June 1864. (Library of Congress)

"Driven back by a storm of artillery and infantry fire"
Colonel Randall L. Gibson, 13th/20th Louisiana Infantry

We were posted on the right of Adams' brigade, the right of the regiment resting near the river, and the two left companies overleaping the rail track. We advanced in line of battle until we reached the houses destroyed by fire, and the point at which the ground swelled into a considerable hill, stretching toward the line of the enemy, and where the river turned off quite abruptly to the right. We then advanced up the ascent, leaving quite an unoccupied space between the right and the river. Ascending the elevated position, I discovered the enemy moving troops rapidly up the river, on our right, and placing them also in ambush in the cornfield on our front. Riding to the rail track, I saw, not more than 50 yards distant, a line of battle of the enemy, using the embankment as a breastwork and to conceal them from our troops on the low ground to our left. The line of battle on the rail track, as the line of battle along the riverbank, was at right angles to our advancing line, and the enemy reserved his fire until the command was flanked.

So soon as I discovered the disposition of the enemy, I rode across the railroad and informed General Adams. It was, however, too late to accomplish a time change in our position. The first fire we received was from the riverbank, and directed upon the infirmary corps of the regiment, posted considerably in our rear. I immediately moved the regiment double-quick by the right flank toward the river, but, finding a front as well as a flanking fire open upon us, I commanded a halt, and determined to contest the field. The right of the regiment stood firm for a few minutes, but under the combined fires gave way. The men naturally faced the direction in which the severest fire came, and this caused some confusion. I felt the necessity of holding our position until the balance of the brigade, already falling back, should pass the point at which the enemy was pressing us on the right. I called upon Major J. E. Austin to form on my line and assist in its defense. In a few moments he disposed his battalion of sharpshooters as I suggested. We were successful in holding the high ground on the right of the railroad until the left portion of the brigade, driven back by a storm of artillery and infantry fire on its front and flank, had reached a point beyond our line.

Colonel Randall Lee Gibson, commanding the consolidated 13th/20th Louisiana Infantry (Liljenquist Collection)

"Our Springfields responded with a hail of death"
Adjutant Edwin Nicar, 15th Indiana Infantry

The order came to move forward to a small cotton field in our right front, to lie down and wait orders to fire. The cotton had been imperfectly picked and bolls with their loads of fleecy whiteness gave us fair concealment from the advancing Rebels. How well I remember the splendid appearance presented by them as they marched to the attack, the stars and bars flung to the breeze, mounted officers and company officers all in place, their lines presenting a solid front and all seemingly determined to emulate and perpetuate the success achieved by their comrades on the right.

But we had been told that our position must be held, that it was necessary to the salvation of the army and we were there to stay. Before reaching our position, the Rebels had to cross the railroad and the deep cut somewhat deranged their formation. Just as they emerged from the cut, we sprang to our feet and the command came, "Ready! Aim! Fire!" Our Springfields responded in a hail of death and after a minute or two of firing at will, the order came, "Fix bayonets! Forward! Charge bayonets! Double quick, march!" And we were at them with a right good will.

For a moment they hesitated, tried to meet our charge, and then broke and ran in utter rout. Never before had I become so excited that I did not know what I was doing. But later I was told that I ran up and down the lines with drawn sword shouting at the top of my voice, "Give them hail Columbia," or something else sounding somewhat similarly and beginning with a big H. Very likely I did act in that manner but I have no recollection of it. Our charge was a magnificent success and the prisoners streamed through our lines in great numbers. My lame ankle was for a time for the time forgotten.

No sooner were the Rebels driven from our front than their artillery again opened on us and we shifted position to the left in the edge of the little piece of woods. Here we sustained another attack which was successfully repelled and about this time our ammunition ran short. The colonel was in despair as no ammunition wagon dared approach our position in consequence of the terrible artillery fire from the heights and it seemed as if we would have to depend on our bayonets.

Captain Joel W. Foster, Co. G, 15ᵗʰ Indiana Infantry was killed in action on the afternoon of December 31, 1862.
(Find-A-Grave)

"*Our broken ranks went back over the fields*"

Maj. Gen. Patrick R. Cleburne, commanding Cleburne's Division

My line advanced steadily, pouring in a deadly fire, and drove the enemy across a small dirt road. That portion of his line opposite Johnson rallied behind a fence on the far side of the dirt road, but was driven from there also, when his whole line disappeared in the cedar woods, which here border the Nashville pike, and were close behind him. Still another line of small arms was immediately directed upon him. He fled back in the woods, leaving the ground in front of Johnson's brigade thickly covered with dead and wounded. Following up their success, our men gained the edge of the cedars Johnson's brigade capturing a battery of Parrott guns and were almost on the Nashville turnpike, in rear of the original center of Rosecrans' army, sweeping with their fire his only line of communication with Nashville.

But it was now after 3 o'clock; my men had had little or no rest the night before; they had been fighting since dawn, without relief, food, or water. At this critical moment the enemy met my thinned ranks with another fresh line of battle, supported by a heavier and closer artillery fire than I had yet encountered. A report also spread, which I believe was true, that we were flanked on the right. This was more than our men could stand. Smith's brigade was driven back in great confusion. Polk's and Johnson's followed. As our broken ranks went back over the fields before the fire of this fresh line, the enemy opened fire on our right flank from several batteries which they had concentrated on an eminence near the railroad, inflicting a heavier loss on Polk's brigade than it had suffered in all the previous fighting of the day.

The division was rallied on the edge of the opposite woods, about 400 yards in rear of the scene of disaster, though some of the men could not be stopped until they reached the Wilkinson pike. Liddell's brigade, en echelon on my extreme left, was not engaged in this last fight and was moved back in good order to the line where the other brigade rallied. Here I reformed my division as rapidly as possible, Polk's brigade on the right, Johnson's in the center, and Liddell's on the left. A fresh supply of ammunition was served out, and I waited in momentary expectation for an advance of the enemy in overwhelming force.

Major General Patrick Ronayne Cleburne
(Library of Congress)

"They scattered and fled without offering resistance"

Colonel Michael Shoemaker, 13th Michigan Infantry

The advance of the Confederates was checked at once and they retreated to the fence between the woods and the open fields, which they lined with their men and which became at once a line of fire blazing at my little regiment. We returned it with such precision and effect as to hold them there but unfortunately our line was much shorter than theirs, they outnumbering us. The overlapping line continued to cautiously advance so that after we had been fighting for about 30 minutes it was reported that the enemy was about to turn our right flank. As there was no appearance of support for us, I ordered the regiment to retire, which was done in good order. Fortunately for us, there was a cedar thicket just in our rear, after passing through which I halted and formed my regiment facing the Confederates who were halting on the line we occupied during the fight and showing signs of hesitation about further advance.

As the enemy had halted and were not following up their advantage, I determined to attack them and I now ordered my regiment to advance, charge, and regain the position. The blood of my men was now up, every man moved forward with a will and as if actuated by a common impulse. As we advanced, every man shouted and yelled to the top of their bent as if confidence of success. As we emerged from the thicket, our men poured a volley of musketry into the ranks of the Confederates who were engaged in examining our dead and wounded and in breaking the muskets lying by them on the ground. The enemy was evidently taken by surprise by our bold and unexpected movement and stunned and confused by the fire of our men delivered almost in their faces. They scattered and fled without offering the least resistance, many of them throwing their arms, some hiding among the rocks or behind trees and others turning and firing upon us as they ran. We gave them no time to recover from their panic but pursued them yelling and shouting so that they might think us thousands instead of hundreds, driving them down out of the woods, across the cleared fields, and into the woods beyond. The whole line was equally affected by the panic and all fled together. We captured 68 prisoners and recaptured the two pieces of cannon lost by Captain Bradley's battery.

Colonel Michael Shoemaker, 13th Michigan Infantry
(Liljenquist Collection)

"The enemy's position was too strong to storm"
Sergeant William D. Rodgers, Co. K, 1st Florida Infantry

The enemy didn't show themselves over on the right and our brigade was ordered to reinforce the center. We added the river about half-leg deep and double-quicked to where they were fighting but we were almost too late as the Yanks had fallen back about two miles to a very strong position and it was getting too late to follow them up. We, that is our right, didn't fire a gun but every other regiment in our brigade got into it pretty deep and suffered severely. We had eight or nine wounded by shells and grape shot but none killed. About dark, was put in the front line and those that had been fighting all day were put in the rear to rest. Our position was in the cedar thicket where the hardest fighting had been. I never saw the like of dead Yanks in my life as there was strewed in that place; there was at least ten Yanks to one of our men.

Colonel William Miller, commanding 1st/3rd Florida Infantry

About 3 p.m., on December 31, we were ordered into line, marched across the river, and formed on a hill in an open field in line of battle, occupying the left of the brigade. The command "forward" was soon given, and on advancing, our front being masked by a regiment, our left was thrown back out of line. This defect in our alignment caused the regiment to diverge to the left, and to enter a cedar forest to the left of the burnt house, the balance of the brigade passing to the right. In charging over this field, we lost several men killed and wounded by the enemy's batteries, which swept the field by an almost enfilading fire. Passing through the cedar, we arrived before the enemy's batteries, and took position on the right of Stewart's brigade, where we were joined by the balance of the brigade. This position of the enemy, supported by heavy batteries, was judged to be too strong to storm; we, therefore, retained our position, skirmishing occasionally with the enemy during that afternoon and the next two following days.

Second Lieutenant Augustus O. McDonnell, Co. K, 1st/3rd Florida Infantry
(William Griffing Collection)

"Many fired over 100 rounds"

Colonel William Grose, commanding Third Brigade

After this, then, between 11 and 12 o'clock, the enemy not appearing in our immediate front, the lines of our forces that had retired or been driven from the right by this time were reformed parallel with the pike, so that the front of the brigade was again changed, so as to assist the brigade of Colonel Hazen in the direction, as formed in the morning. The 24th Ohio and 36th Indiana were soon thrown forward near the railroad and had a terrible conflict with the enemy. Here Colonel Frederick Jones and Major Henry Terry both fell and were carried off the field in a dying condition.

Each regiment of the brigade, from this until night closed the awful scene, alternately took its part in holding the position that we occupied in the morning. The enemy having gained the heavy cedar woods to the right, where we first took position in the morning, it became necessary to so change our position as to not be in reach of small-arms from that woodland; hence, at nightfall the center of the front line of the brigade laid on the pike and diagonally across the same, fronting to the southeast our left resting at the right of the lines of General Wood's division. We were then a little retired, and the center of the brigade about 250 yards to the left of where we commenced in the morning. We ceased fighting for the night, with the front lines on the pike. During the day each of the regiments, having exhausted, had to replenish, their ammunition, many of them having fired over 100 rounds.

When Major Isaac Kinley, of the 36th Indiana, fell, nearly at the commencement in the morning, the command devolved upon Captain Pyrrhus Woodward: and upon the fall of Colonel Frederick Jones and Major Henry Terry, of the 24th Ohio, Captain Enoch Weller was left in command. Although I was at Shiloh and commanded in that battle at the head of General Buell's army, and fought throughout that battle with that army, yet this battle, the last day of the old year, was by far the most terrible and bloody in my command that I have ever witnessed.

Colonel William Grose, formerly 36th Indiana Infantry
(Library of Congress)

"We did not pursue them farther"

Colonel Joseph B. Palmer, commanding Palmer's Brigade

At noon on Wednesday, December 31, I was ordered by General Breckinridge [as was also General Preston] across Stone's River, to the left wing of our general line of battle. Arriving there, we were immediately ordered to move upon the enemy's position just west of Cowan's residence. In this charge General Preston was on the right, while I was directed to form upon and move with his left, and, during the movement, to effect a general change of direction of my line to the right, so as to support the right brigade and flank the enemy.

The several regiments of my brigade moved gallantly and steadily forward in this charge, although exposed to a terrible fire from Yankee artillery for a distance of 400 yards across an open and unprotected field. The movement was successful on our part. The Federal forces abandoned their ground, retreating westwardly back on the main body of their troops, where their position was strongly protected by embankments thrown up in the construction of the railroad, some natural elevations of the ground, and the cover of their artillery. On these accounts we did not pursue them farther.

In this action both the men and officers of the brigade behaved with most becoming courage and gallantry, displaying a high degree of unfaltering determination and bravery, now mentioned alike in justice to them and with the utmost satisfaction to myself.

Colonel (later General) Joseph B. Palmer, the former mayor of Murfreesboro, would be wounded during Breckinridge's assault on the afternoon of January 2, 1863. Palmer would survive the wound only to be wounded again at Chickamauga, Jonesboro, and Bentonville in March 1865.
(Rick Baumgartner Collection)

"A pell-mell, helter-skelter panic"
Captain James Stinchcomb, Co. B, 17th Ohio Infantry

When about two miles from the field, we met a continuous stream of sneakers and skulkers flying in a perfect panic, reporting the day lost to us and our army cut to pieces. They were in the utmost confusion: privates, lieutenants, captains, and even colonels in the wildest panic; footmen, cavalrymen, wagons, batteries running pell-mell, helter-skelter. They were not less than 3,000 in this panic, all flying. I tell you it looked gloomy to our three regiments, yet we were formed in battle line on a commanding point by Colonel Moses Walker, commanding the brigade, in as good order as if we were on battalion drill. It soon became evident that it was simply a panic created by a pack of cowards and scared men, whereupon Colonel Walker ordered Captain McQuilkin of his staff and me to stop them. We took a small detail and, in a few minutes, had a large number of them reorganized. Heavy cannonading commenced again within 400 yards and after waiting a few minutes, one of General Thomas' aides arrived ordering us to the field with all possible speed, informing us that our men were driving the Rebels on the left and all they needed was some support on the right to save the whole field. Our boys moved up eager for the fray.

In about ten minutes we met another panic that beggars description: 500 wagons, the drivers whipping and swearing, some bare-headed, others without coats or shoes, all scared to death. Here was another wild rush of cavalry and footmen (there is heavy musketry firing on my left now, not 400 yards distant). In another panic, reporting 30,000 Rebels at their heels with heavy cavalry forces in full charge. Our three regiments, the 17th, 31st, and 38th Ohio were immediately formed in squares, with a section of the battery in each square. I was ordered to stop the wagons and thereby save the panic from being continued and oh, save me from such another job, I never want to try it again. The scared officers appeared as maniacs. Wagons crowded up until they were eight or ten deep. After drawing my revolver and presenting it to two or three officers and got them to see our squares, they assisted and we soon got the train stopped and after telling the drivers it was only a panic and not to be scared.

Captain Ezra Ricketts, Co. F, 17th Ohio Infantry would be killed in action at the Battle of Chickamauga nine months later.
(Larry M. Strayer Collection)

"The position should be carried, held, and strongly fortified"

Major William D. Pickett, assistant inspector general, Hardee's Corps

On the 2nd of January, General William J. Hardee with myself passed along the Confederate position to the crossing of Stones River and met General Leonidas Polk alone. While a private conversation was had between the two, the party had crossed the river and soon were met by General John C. Breckinridge. During this time, it appeared to be the design of these officers to make a reconnaissance with a view to a movement on the Federal left flank as it was to be expected that he had a force on that side of the river to guard it. Before much had been accomplished in the reconnaissance General Hardee was recalled hurriedly to his line by a staff officer; turning to General Breckinridge, he said, "I must return but will leave Pickett here to represent me." After the Federal position had been thoroughly reconnoitered, a message came from General Bragg for General Breckinridge to report at his temporary headquarters a few hundred yards in the rear on the riverbank. My impression is that General Bragg had already determined to make the attack as he at once commenced explaining the order of attack.

Prefacing his orders with the remark that as his division had not been much engaged in the battle of December 31, it had been selected for this important movement. These remarks did not appear to me at the time to be made in any invidious or critical sense as afterwards charged. Bragg's orders to Breckinridge were that a vigorous attack on the position just reconnoitered should be carried, held, and strongly fortified, having in view positions for four field batteries. Besides three batteries from his own division, he had assigned Captain Felix Robertson's battery from Polk's corps. The hour of the attack was to be about 4 o'clock, the signal being a discharge of four pieces of artillery in quick succession. The impression appeared to be that with an attack at that hour, if successful, the enemy would not attempt to retake it that night giving us ample time to fortify. The balance of the army at the signal were to make demonstrations with artillery and otherwise along the whole front. These instructions were given in my hearing about noon on January 2. Breckinridge began at once to make the necessary preparations for carrying out the order of battle.

Major General John Cabell Breckinridge depicted as Vice President of the United States in 1860.
(Library of Congress)

"I was wounded in four places"

Sergeant John H. Purvis, Co. B, 51st Ohio Infantry

On the evening of the 2nd instant, we had a severe engagement on the left where our brigade was stationed. The enemy came upon us in overwhelming numbers. They came swarming in masses, not in columns, and our ranks melted away before them like snow on a spring morning. We fought desperately, but all was of no avail, and the order was given to retreat. But I did not hear it amid the noise of battle and continued to load and fire until the Rebels were almost upon me. Just as I had brought my gun up to fire the sixth time, a ball struck me on the top of my head, knocking me over on my back, but the wound was not deep and I quickly sprung to my feet, discharged my musket, and loaded again. But the blood streamed over my face and into my eyes so that I could not see. Then I turned around to go behind a tree a short distance off, carrying my gun with me. But no sooner had I reached the tree than a ball entered my left leg just above the ankle. This brought me down to my knees, and just as I fell another rifle ball struck me in the lower part of my bowels, and a buck shot hit me on the left knee but this last did not go very deep. Thus, I was wounded in four places and I then thought the wound in my bowels was mortal. I was glad to lie down by the tree, faint from the loss of blood which flowed freely from my head and leg.

On came the enemy with shouts and yells, trampling over me. What my feelings were I leave you to imagine. I cared not so much for myself, though my wounds were frightful; hundreds of my comrades were as badly or worse hurt than I was; but to hear the cursed Rebels shout victory was galling in the extreme. Their triumph was short-lived, however, for our men soon rallied; reinforcements soon arrived, and 50 pieces of artillery opened on the Rebel masses. The effect was terrific. The heavens seemed rent with the awful volume of sound which burst from those 50 cannons. The forest trees were shattered to splinters and the earth was torn up by the iron storm. The Rebels were hurled back in dismay, hundreds falling to rise no more. All who could escaped and back they fled in wild confusion, throwing away their guns and everything else they carried and uttering bitter curses in their flight. It did my heart good to see them run, closely pursued by our men.

*Sergeant (later Lieutenant) John H. Purvis, Co. B, 51ˢᵗ Ohio Infantry
(Brad & Donna Pruden Collection)*

"We were unable to hold our ground"
Sergeant Dan E. Turney, Co. G, 2nd Kentucky Infantry (C.S.A.)

All was quiet until about 3:30 p.m. when General Breckinridge moved his division out to attack the enemy who had crossed the river on our right and taken a strong position in the woods. General Hanson's brigade was the left wing of the front line, a Tennessee brigade on the right wing, two other brigades forming the second line of battle. Our orders were to move upon the woods occupied by the enemy at a double quick and to rush upon them at a charge bayonet. The orders were strictly obeyed but there not being room for the line to maneuver between the bends of the river, some confusion arose from being crowded en masse. Nothing daunted, all went in with a yell and drove the enemy before them in the wildest confusion. The slaughter was great, many being left dead and wounded on the field and many killed in the fight, several hundred are taken prisoners, some cross the river and many shelter themselves under the cliffs. The rout was complete and our loss thus far was trifling. The orders were to halt at the edge of the woods beyond the range of the enemy's grape and canister but the race was too exciting and our boys too impetuous; we could not hold and must still pursue. As well might you ask the winged lightnings to quit their celestial course or the planetary worlds to change their orbits as to bid the Southern patriot to withdraw from the slaughter of the destroyers of peace. No, revenge was in his heart and vengeance was in his eye and he sped recklessly on regardless of his own safety's fate.

Having advanced as far as possible for the river left us in the form of a "V," we halted when the enemy opened several masked batteries upon us at a distance of 200 yards, they advanced several divisions of infantry which poured upon us an enfilade fire. With the river in front, we could not advance to storm their batteries nor could we reach them with our small arms from the low position we occupied. We were being flanked on our right, there was no alternative but to fall back but there was a general rally as soon as we were beyond the reach of their grape and canister when the enemy was checked. We accomplished the object of our battle, driving the enemy across the river but were unable to hold the ground taken from him owing to his strong commanding position.

Brigadier General Roger Weightman Hanson of Kentucky died of a wound sustained leading the Orphan Brigade in its January 2nd attack which he believed was pure folly. (Library of Congress)

"Few men keep their presence of mind when balls cut their hair"

Adjutant Erasmus Darwin Thomas, 86th Indiana Infantry

Breckinridge massed a force in close column and charged across an open field in our front with a design to capture our division which was alone across the river. Then came what is said to be the hardest fighting that two armies can do. Bullets flew by the bushel from artillery and musketry. 52 of our guns opened upon the poor fellows; no field was ever so blue with flying lead. Very many of my friends and those who I esteemed on account of their bravery are among the dead. One of the staff fell badly wounded and had his horse killed very near me. Colonel Fyffe was thrown from his horse and dragged some distance. I was with him all the time on the field but all the little flying deaths missed me.

Any man on a horse was a target for the sharpshooters and any group of horsemen for the artillery. You can form no idea of such a battle without being on the field. Why you never heard such a noise! Any amount of thunder won't compare with it. But when you are in the midst of the firing, you don't notice the big noise so much as the meanest of all sounds continually going past your ear with their whiz, zip, spat, and thug as one of the Minies hits some poor fellow and sends him to the ground. I don't know why I was not hit, for it seemed to me that everybody was shooting at me and every time I saw a man fall at my side, I thought the ball that was to knock me off was right at hand. Even after the hardest of the fight was over and I thought myself safe here would come a big shell across the country and tearing up the ground, fall right by the side of me.

A line of Rebels marching through the woods is the ugliest sight I ever saw. When a desperate charge is to be made such as was made upon us by Breckinridge, they form their columns and place a strong guard in the rear to shoot every man who attempts to fall back or leave the ranks. The great trouble in battles is to keep men together; so many of them get confused and don't shoot with good effect, but it is not to be wondered at. Very few men keep their presence of mind when balls are cutting their hair and tearing their clothes.

Private George E. Armer, Co. B, 86th Indiana Infantry was killed in action at Stones River.
(Find-A-Grave)

"The conflict was bloody and desperate in the extreme"

Captain Theodorick "Tod" Carter, Co. H, 20th Tennessee Infantry

*L*ate in the evening of Friday, General Breckinridge's division made one of the most brilliant charges of the war. The enemy had massed a heavy force in the cedar forest north of Stones River near the Lebanon Road and were menacing this wing which was held by a single division. Towards the close of evening, they left a large reserve in this strongly entrenched position and advanced on us with a long heavy line of infantry and artillery, overlapping our command by a strong brigade.

General Breckinridge charged them, and the conflict ensued, bloody and desperate in the extreme. Their artillery opened upon us a most terrific fire and our forces melted away like night shadows before the break of morning, but they struggled on in face of the fiery sleet, like gods for their altars. For an hour the demons of hell seemed to have met in wild, blood-drunken revelry. The enemy finally gave way and our boys dashed upon the like a tigress to her bloody banquet and drove them howling through woods and fields and over the hills to the river and across the river to their den, their reserve. And then, notwithstanding the statement of your correspondent, withdrew quietly and without opposition. The enemy fought bravely but they met men fighting for their homes and their little ones and notwithstanding their superior force, were repulsed and driven back in slaughter. The ground was literally blue with their dead and dying. Our thinned ranks attest to their courage with a melancholy eloquence.

Many of our best and highest spirits fell upon that field. Lieutenant Colonel Labenda, the very soul of gallantry, is still there. Spring will bring her sweetest flowers to that sacred spot. Our loss was heavy. As an instance, the 20th Tennessee with less than 400 men in the fight lost 158! We repulsed them, yes, we whipped them everywhere and our boys were willing to settle the war in sight of Murfreesboro. Why we retreated some future Columbus must discover.

Private Francis Marion Battle, Co. B, 20ᵗʰ Tennessee Infantry
(Liljenquist Collection)

"A charge right up to the river's edge"
First Lt. Robert S. Dilworth, Co. I, 21st Ohio Infantry

On Friday afternoon, the Rebels made a charge on our left center. We were ordered out then and took our position near the river's side, lying down in mass. The regiment had not been in this position for more than half an hour when the storm of battle commenced. It lasted about 20 minutes, the Rebels coming on eight columns deep and forcing us back in confusion. On swept the tide of battle. Pell-mell, hurry-scurry, came our troops, hotly pursued by the advancing Rebel columns. The 99th Ohio broke across the river and came near running over us. When they had finally passed through our ranks, Colonel [James] Neibling in his sonorous voice cried out, "Attention!" The whole regiment sprang to their feet in an instant with their arms gripped, ready for the oncoming assault of the Rebel forces and the coming struggle.

The Rebels charged up the river's edge and Colonel Neibling cried out "Deploy into line on the fifth company!" We were in our places quicker than it takes to tell it, and our next command was to lie down. Then we commenced to pour a withering fire into their advancing ranks which caused them to begin to fall back. Colonel Jim then rode out and in a voice that sounded above the din of battle, cried out "Charge!" And charge it was, right up to the river's bank, amidst a terrible swarm of iron and lead. The Rebels began to retreat in dismay as we charged across the river. Thrice was their flag and banner cut down and thrice did it wave over the heads of the retreating butternuts. At length, they were felled to no more rise in secession, many of them falling into the hands of the 74th Ohio.

We then charged upon this battery which was placed in a woods across an open cornfield about 60 rods in width, right into the face of its murderous fire, a monster battery of five English guns. Yet we must go or lose the prize while it belched forth its missiles of death which fell upon us like rain in our midst. Just when we were within about 50 yards of the doomed battery (which still did its work well), we heard a shout to our right and then came a stream of fire at a distance of about 30 yards from the noble prize. The Rebels skedaddled, leaving their battery in our hands, and nighttime soon brought an end to the bloody battle.

First Lieutenant Robert S. Dilworth, Co. I, 21st Ohio was later killed in action near Kennesaw Mountain, Georgia in June 1864. (Robert Van Dorn Collection)

"The brigade retired in some confusion"

Brig. Gen. Gideon J. Pillow, commanding Palmer's Brigade

At the signal for the movements to commence, I ordered my line to advance. The entire line moved forward in beautiful order across the strip of woods and open field, driving the enemy's skirmishers and sharpshooters before it, and at the distance of about 300 yards receiving the fire of the main body of the enemy's infantry, hitherto concealed from view. This fire developed a large body of the enemy's sharpshooters in a body of thick woods to the right of the position now occupied by my advanced line. I immediately ordered Lieutenant R.W. Anderson to bring up his battery and to drive them out of the wood.

The two batteries, confronting each other, kept up an exceedingly hot fire for about fifteen minutes, when my infantry, pressing the enemy's infantry, forced it to retire into and then from a thicket of woods which skirted the bluff; the enemy's body of sharpshooters and battery retreated precipitately from the woods on the right toward the river bluff. I now ordered the infantry to press the enemy and clear the bluff, while I advanced Anderson's battery, and with it occupied the woods from which the enemy's artillery had been driven. This order was promptly executed, the bluff cleared, the enemy's infantry taking shelter under the bluff and in a deep ravine running obliquely into the river.

My infantry having thus advanced as far as was possible on account of the bluff and having forced many broken portions of the enemy's forces across and through the river, his artillery having retired down the river in the direction of the ford, my fire ceased, and the work seemed completed. In a few moments afterward I discovered a large body of the enemy moving rapidly up the river on my side, turning my right wing. It advanced rapidly and opened upon the flank and rear of my force. Simultaneously the enemy's artillery and infantry in the front of my position, and on the opposite side of the river, opened fire upon my front, uncovered as it was, on the open bluff on the right bank. It retired in some confusion, but with as little as could have been expected when suddenly surprised by movements of the enemy's fresh forces, which could not have been foreseen, and which we had not the means of meeting.

Brigadier General Gideon Johnson Pillow
(Library of Congress)

"58 guns opened fire on the enemy"

Captain John Mendenhall, chief of artillery, Left Wing

About 4 p.m., while riding along the pike with General Crittenden, we heard heavy firing of artillery and musketry on the left. We at once rode briskly over, and, arriving upon the hill near the ford, saw our infantry retiring before the enemy. The general asked me if I could not do something to relieve Colonel Beatty with my guns. Captain Swallow had already opened with his battery. I ordered Lieutenant Parsons to move a little forward and open with his guns; then rode back to bring up Lieutenant Estep, with his 8th Indiana Battery. Meeting Captain Morton, with his brigade of Pioneers, he asked for advice, and I told him to move briskly forward with his brigade, and send his battery to the crest of the hill, near the batteries already engaged. The 8th Indiana Battery took position to the right of Lieutenant Parsons.

Seeing that Lieutenant Osburn was in position (between Lieutenants Parsons and Estep), I rode to Lieutenant Stevens (26th Pennsylvania Battery), and directed him to change front, to fire to the left and open fire; and then to Captain Standart, and directed him to move to the left with his pieces; and he took position covering the ford. I found that Captain Bradley had anticipated my wishes, and had changed front to fire to the left, and opened upon the enemy; this battery was near the railroad. Lieutenant Livingston's (3rd Wisconsin) battery (which was across the river) opened upon the advancing enemy, and continued to fire until he thought he could no longer maintain his position, when he crossed over, one section at a time, and opened fire again. The firing ceased about dark.

During this terrible encounter of little more than an hour in duration, forty-three pieces of artillery, belonging to the left wing, the Board of Trade Battery of six guns, and the batteries of General Negley's division, about nine guns, making a total of about fifty-eight pieces, opened fire upon the enemy. The enemy soon retired, our troops following;

Major General Thomas Leonidas Crittenden, commanding Left Wing, Army of the
Cumberland
(Author's Collection)

"We nobly held our ground"

Colonel John G. Coltart, commanding Loomis's brigade

The next morning (Saturday) the 19th Alabama, 25th Alabama, and Captain

Yancey's sharpshooters in conjunction with two Mississippi regiments (9th and 10th) were ordered to recover a position lost the previous evening. After a few minutes of shelling by our batteries, the infantry gallantly charged the position, driving the enemy therefrom and captured a lieutenant colonel, one lieutenant, and 13 privates. The position being threatened, the 1st Louisiana and 39th Alabama regiments were thrown into the woods to support the troops already there. The Mississippi regiments were afterwards withdrawn.

Just at nightfall, the enemy made a strong effort to retake the position and succeeded in driving the 1st Louisiana and 39th Alabama from that portion of the wood held by them, but it was again recovered by the two Mississippi regiments who came to their aid. The 19th and 25th Alabama nobly held their ground and repulsed the enemy.

Colonel John G. Coltart, 26th Alabama Infantry
(Stan Hutson Collection)

"Our situation is by no means an enviable one"

Lt. Col. James Maynard Shanklin, 42nd Indiana Infantry

It was on this night about 10:30 p.m. that our regiment was ordered out on picket with instructions to keep advancing and feel the enemy's lines. This I did as well as I could. The men had eaten nothing for two days and it rained steadily all Friday night so that all of us were wet through. At the break of day, the enemy commenced shelling us and throwing grape. The men could do nothing of course except leave the woods. I was indifferent and worn out and after making an effort to keep up, I found that I could not do so. The enemy's skirmishers supported by a whole brigade soon surrounded Lieutenant John Scammehorn, myself, and eight of our men. I ordered the men not to fire as it would be only a useless resistance and surrendered.

My surrender in my opinion saved many men of the regiment. The Confederates seemed perfectly satisfied and made no attempt to pursue the men and their cannons ceased firing. They gathered around me and asked my rank which I gave. Had they followed to the edge of the woods, they could have shot down our men by the dozen as they passed over the open field. I was immediately taken inside of their lines and placed under guard. Several officers treated me very kindly including Major Wall, Captain Phil Allen of Henderson, Kentucky, Lieutenant James W. Nichol, and John Bell, Junior, son of John Bell who ran for the Presidency, all of the last three loaning me some money. I shall always remember them.

I have indulged in a great many vain regrets since taken that I did not make more of an effort to get away. The truth of the matter is I felt so utterly worn out and my feet were so very sore that I was almost indifferent whether I was taken or shot. After leaving Chattanooga, we were brought to Atlanta, a very pretty town what little I have seen of it. Our situation here, however, is by no means an enviable one. The fare is very hard, only cornbread and beef but it all is they have. The prison has been uncomfortably full, 60 men being confined to one room and 12 in another. I believe everything is done that they can do, but they are not able to do much.

Lieutenant Colonel James M. Shanklin, 42nd Indiana Infantry
(Find-A-Grave)

"I hope General Bragg will break us up"

Sergeant Isaac Wark, Co. E, 1st Louisiana Regular Infantry

I carried the colors of the regiment during the four last days. We were kept very busy while in Murfreesboro, being on the provost marshal's guard we were on guard every other day and when the Yanks advanced, we were sent to the front. We went into the fight with 24 officers and 231 men and had 87 men killed and wounded besides some 30 missing, supposed to have been taken prisoners. The Yanks came near finishing the regiment on the evening of the third day. They played a Yankee trick on us. We were in a small strip of woods about halfway between our lines and the enemy was on picket duty. And the Yanks wishing to ascertain our positions sent over a flag of truce to recover the body of some officer that had been killed the day before. In the ambulance that accompanied the flag was an artillery officer taking items as we afterwards found to our sorrow. For as soon as they reached their lines, they commenced shelling us at a terrible rate. One of the first shells struck Lieutenant Colonel Farrar; several of the men were also wounded. During the shelling, a heavy line of battle advanced on us some 6,000-7,000 men strong and was not discovered until within about 30 feet of us. Those that were able got up and dusted or, in military parlance, fell back to the regiments that were supporting us. When they saw us coming back, they immediately broke and ran back to the breastworks with the exception of the 19th Alabama which, along with what was left of ours, held the enemy in check until the 9th and 41st Mississippi advanced and supported us as we drove the Yanks back to their breastworks about midnight.

We commenced the work of evacuation and marched the balance of that night and all next day. I can tell you we have suffered a great deal during the last two weeks. I don't know what they intend to do with us. We are scarcely a hundred men strong and there don't seem to be much of a prospect of filling the regiment up. I hope General Bragg will break us up and put us into some other regiment so that we might get clear of these officers. I never had a very good opinion of them at any time but since the fight they have become worse than they ever were. They are as cowardly a set of men as could be found. They were all drunk during the fight and with one or two exceptions could not be seen during any of the heavy fighting.

Major General Jones M. Withers
(Library of Congress)

"The enemy abandoned the field"

Colonel John Beatty, commanding Second Brigade

The Rebels hold a strip of woods in our immediate front, and we get into a lively skirmish with them. About nightfall, General Rousseau desires me to get two regiments in readiness, and, as soon as it becomes quite dark, charge upon and clean out the woods in our front. I selected the 3rd Ohio and 88th Indiana for this duty, and at the appointed time we form line in the open field in front of Guenther's battery, and as we start, the battery commences to shell the woods. As we get nearer the objective point, I put the men on the double quick.

The Rebels, discovering our approach, open a heavy fire, but in the darkness shoot too high. The blaze of their guns reveals their exact position to us. We reach the rude log breastworks behind which they are standing and grapple with them. Colonel Humphrey receives a severe thrust from a bayonet; others are wounded, and some killed. It is pitch dark under the trees. Some of Guenther's shells fall short and alarm the men. Unable to find either staff officer or orderly, I ride back and request him to elevate his guns.

Returning, I find my troops blazing away with great energy; but, so far as I can discover, their fire is not returned. It is difficult, however, in the noise, confusion, and darkness, to direct their movements, and impossible to stop the firing. In the meantime, a new danger threatens. Spear's Tennesseeans have been sent to support us, probably without any definite instructions. They are, most of them, raw troops, and, becoming either excited or alarmed at the terrible racket in the woods, deliver scattering shots in our rear. I ride back and urge them either to cease firing or move to the left, go forward and look after our flank. One regiment does move as directed; but the others are immovable, and it is with great difficulty that I succeed in making them understand that in firing they are more likely to injure friends than foes.

Fortunately, soon after this, the ammunition of the 3rd and 88th becoming exhausted, the firing in the woods ceases, and as the enemy has already abandoned the field, the affair ends. I try to find General Rousseau to report results, but cannot; and so, worn out with fatigue and excitement, lie down for another night.

Colonel John Beatty
(Larry M. Strayer Collection)

A metal silhouette depicting a Union infantryman from Colonel John F. Miller's rests among the limestone formations near tour stop No. 2 at Stones River National Battlefield.

Bibliography

Beatty, John. *The Citizen-Soldier: Memoirs of a Civil War Volunteer.* Cincinnati: Wilstach, Baldwin, & Co., 1879

Bradshaw, George E., Letter in author's private collection

Breidenthal, Henry, Letter from *Ohio State Journal*, January 24, 1863

Buck, Martin, Letter from *Highland Weekly News*, February 12, 1863

Butler, Marvin B. *My Story of the Civil War and the Underground Railroad.* Huntington: The United Brethren Publishing Establishment, 1914

Carter, Tod, Letter from *Chattanooga Daily Rebel*, January 15, 1863

Dennis, Charles Barney, Memoirs of Civil War Service, Rutherford B. Hayes Memorial Library, Fremont, Ohio

Dilworth, Robert S., Letter from *Pittsburgh Commercial Gazette*, November 16, 1896

Downs, Noah W., Letter from *Howard Tribune*, February 12, 1863

Ellis, Ezekiel John, Memoir, Stones River National Battlefield Park Archives

Garternicht, Frederick, Letter from *Oquawka Spectator*, January 29, 1863

Harder, William Henry Harder, Memoirs. Tennessee State Library and Archives

Hastings, Adoniram Judson, Letter from *Union County Star and Lewisburg Chronicle,* January 27, 1863

Haymond, Henry, Letter, Stones River National Battlefield Park Archives

Hinman, Wilbur F., Papers, Western Reserve Historical Society

Houghtaling, Charles, Letter from *Illinois State Journal,* January 12, 1863

McDearman, William J. "Private M'Dearman at Murfreesboro, *Confederate Veteran*, Vol. 9

Manderson, Charles F. *The Twin Seven Shooters.* New York: F. Tennyson Neely, 1902

Maple, Charles H., Letter from *Fulton County Ledger*, January 27, 1863

Maxwell, Thomas J., Letter from *Delaware Gazette*, February 6, 1863

Mayer, Simon, Diary, Stones River National Battlefield Park Archives

Mitchell, John Lendrum. *In Memoriam: John Lendrum Mitchell.* Milwaukee: 1906

Nicar, Edwin. "A Reminiscence of Stone's River," *National Tribune,* June 13, 1895

Pickett, William B. "Reminiscences of Murfreesboro." *Confederate Veteran*, Vol. 16

Preston, William E.M., memoir from private collection

Purvis, John H., Letter from *Tuscarawas Advocate*, February 6, 1863

Reed, Frank, Letter from *Ohio Democrat*, January 30, 1863

Rodgers, William D., Letter, Stones River National Battlefield Park Archives

Ross, Tobias, Letter from *Cincinnati Daily Commercial*, January 29, 1863

Rugeley, Helen J.H., editor. *Batchelor-Turner Letters, 1861-1864*. Austin: The Steck Co., 1961

Sallee, Lycurgus A., Letter, Stones River National Battlefield Park Archives

Scott, Launcelot L., Diary, Stones River National Battlefield Park Archives

Seay, Samuel. "A Private at Stone River." *Southern Bivouac,* August 1885

Shanklin, James M., Letter from McCutchan, Kenneth P., editor. *Dearest Lizzie-the Civil War seen through the eyes of Lieutenant Colonel James Maynard Shanklin*. Evansville: Friends of the Willard Library Press, 1988

Smith, Lanny K. *The Stones River Campaign: 26 December 1862-5 January 1863. Army of Tennessee*. Lanny Smith, 2010

Shoemaker, Michael. "Narrative of Colonel Michael Shoemaker," 1878 Annual Meeting of the Pioneer Society of Michigan

Stinchcomb, James, Letter from *Lancaster Gazette*, January 15, 1863

Stuart, Almon, Letter from *St. Joseph Valley Register,* February 5, 1863

Thomas, Erasmus D., Letter in Merrill, Catharine. *The Soldier of Indiana in the War for the Union, Vol. II.* Indianapolis: Merrill & Co., 1869

Tingle, James, Memoir. Historical Society of Vandalia-Butler, Ohio

Tunnell, James T., "Texans in the Battle of Murfreesboro." *Confederate Veteran,* Vol. 16

Turney, Dan E., Diary, Stones River National Battlefield Park Archives

Walker, Cornelius Irvine. *Rolls and Historical Sketch of the Tenth Regiment So. Ca. Volunteers in the Army of the Confederate States.* Charleston: Walker, Evans, and Cogswell, 1881

The War of the Rebellion: A Compilation of the Official Records of the Union and Confederate Armies. 128 vols. Washington, D.C., 1880-1901

Wark, Isaac F., Letter, Stones River National Battlefield Park Archives

Weir, James K., Letter, Stones River National Battlefield Park Archives

Woodruff, George H. *History of the One Hundredth; or Will County Regiment. Fifteen Years Ago: or the Patriotism of Will County, Designed to Preserve the names and memory of Will County Soldiers.* Joliet: James Goodspeed, 1876

Index of Accounts and Images

Index of Accounts and Images by Unit

www.ingramcontent.com/pod-product-compliance
Lightning Source LLC
Chambersburg PA
CBHW040148010726
47475CB00039B/490